Bamboo Among the Oaks

Bamboo

Among the Oaks

Contemporary Writing
by Hmong Americans

∞

Edited by MAI NENG MOUA

BOREALIS
BOOKS

Borealis Books is an imprint of the Minnesota Historical Society Press.

www.borealisbooks.org

The Minnesota Historical Society Press is a member of the Association of American University Presses.

Manufactured in the United States of America

10 9 8 7 6 5 4 3

♾ The paper used in this publication meets the minimum requirements of the American National Standard for Information Sciences—Permanence for Printed Library Materials, ANSI Z39.48-1984.

International Standard Book Number
ISBN 13: 978-0-87351-437-8 (paper)
ISBN 10: 0-87351-437-8 (paper)

Library of Congress Cataloging-in-Publication Data

Bamboo among the oaks : contemporary writing by Hmong Americans / edited by Mai Neng Moua.
      p. cm.
ISBN 0-87351-436-X
      (cloth ed. : alk. paper)
ISBN 0-87351-437-8
      (paper ed. : alk. paper)
   1. American literature—
      Hmong American authors.
   2. Hmong Americans—
      Literary collections.
   3. American literature—
      20th century.
   4. Hmong Americans.
   I. Moua, Mai Neng, 1974–

PS508.H63 B36 2002
810.9′895942—dc21

                           2002004320

"Endstage" is excerpted from an essay that appeard in the Minnesota Center for Health Care Ethics' publication *Cross-cultural Case Narratives Involving Hmong Families and Health Care Professionals* (Vanderbilt University Press, 2002).

Bamboo Among the Oaks

Acknowledgments

I thank the Minnesota Historical Society Press for giving me this opportunity to edit *Bamboo Among the Oaks*. I thank the staff (Greg Britton, Ann Regan, and Shannon M. Pennefeather) for working tirelessly with me to make this an incredible anthology.

This anthology would not have been possible without the assistance, consultation, and encouragement of the following members of the *Paj Ntaub Voice* Advisory & Editorial Board:

> May Lee
> Mitch Ogden
> Mayli Vang
> Xai Xiong
> Naly Yang
> Peter Yang

These volunteers were deeply immersed in the whole process, from the call for submissions to deciding on a title, and through lengthy deliberations as we made selections. Thank you for your honesty, commitment, and hard work.

I thank all the contributors who have willingly shared their stories. I thank those folks who gave me valuable support, criticism, and feedback: Alex Lubet, Mitch Ogden, Bryan Thao Worra, Yer Moua Xiong, and Dr. Kou Yang.

Finally, I thank my family and friends for their undying support.

MAI NENG MOUA

Bamboo Among the Oaks

Introduction

Power consists in the ability to make others inhabit your story of their reality.
          Philip Gourevitch, *We Wish to Inform You That*
          Tomorrow We Will Be Killed with Our Families

[W]hen we speak
we are afraid
our words will not be heard
nor welcomed
but when we are silent
we are still afraid.
So it is better to speak
          audre lorde, "A Litany for Survival"

How much Hmong history and culture must I provide before
we can have a conversation about Hmong literature? This is
a question that I as a Hmong writer often contemplate. Sometimes it feels like an added burden, one not imposed on writers
who are white and from the majority culture. But as a Hmong
writer, I must engage the question in order to have dialogue.
How then do I answer it without painting myself and every
other Hmong writer with one stroke?

This little I can tell you briefly: No one knows for certain
the origin of the Hmong people. Mention of the Hmong is found
in four- or five-thousand-year-old Chinese documents. Southern
China still has the largest Hmong population in the world.
In the 1800s some of the Hmong migrated into Southeast Asia
(Cambodia, Laos, Thailand, and Vietnam). In Laos (home to
most of the Hmong who eventually settled in the United States),
the Hmong were self-sufficient farmers who lived in mountain-
top villages.

The Hmong started arriving in the United States in the
mid-1970s as a result of the Vietnam War. Most of the Hmong
men were soldiers of the Second Military Region of the Royal

Lao Army, led by General Vang Pao. Hmong soldiers collaborated with the Central Intelligence Agency to defend their own territory and way of life and to rescue American pilots downed along the Ho Chi Minh Trail. After the Americans pulled out of Southeast Asia, the Communist Pathet Lao targeted the Hmong for destruction. Many fled into Thailand, where they lived in refugee camps before resettling in Argentina, Australia, Canada, France, Germany, and the United States.*

According to the U.S. census for the year 2000, there are more than 169,000 Hmong in the United States. The five states with the largest Hmong population are California, Minnesota, Wisconsin, North Carolina, and Michigan. An estimated 40,000 Hmong live in Minnesota, ranking it second in this list. The Hmong in Minnesota are concentrated in the St. Paul–Minneapolis area. In fact, St. Paul has the most Hmong residents of any city in the world.

The Hmong culture is based on oral traditions—knowledge handed down verbally from father to son and mother to daughter. The Hmong did not have a writing system until the 1950s, when Catholic missionaries developed the Romanized Popular Alphabet (RPA) to translate the Bible into Hmong—or *Hmoob*, as it is spelled in the RPA system. At about the same time, a Hmong man by the name of Shong Lue Yang developed *Ntawv Phaj Hauj*, a script made up of characters dissimilar to those used in any other written language. Although there were at least eight known writing systems developed in the 1950s, RPA is the most commonly used today. To our knowledge, there is no earlier tradition of written Hmong literature.

Because the traditional Hmong arts have not been written down (offering no convenient texts for historians and anthropologists to pore over), some may think they do not exist.

* See notes beginning on page 203.

This is not true. Art in the Hmong community is all around. In China, Laos, and Thailand, we Hmong lived our art. It was in the hand-sewn costumes we wore to the Hmong New Year; it was in the *kwv txhiaj* we sang at the farms; it was in the hoes and knives we used; it was in the religious rituals we performed; it was in the houses in which we lived. It was such an integral part of our everyday lives that there was no separation between what was art and what was culture.

Traditional Hmong arts include oral arts, such as *paj haum, kwv txhiaj,* and *dab neeg*; textile art such as *paj ntaub;* the making, dyeing, and weaving of hemp into clothing; the smithing or metal-working of knives, guns, axes, and farm tools; the construction of musical instruments such as *qeej,* mouth harps, flutes, and *xiv xaum* or *raj nkauj nog;* the creation of jewelry, including earrings, bracelets, and necklaces; the architectural construction of Hmong homes; the making of toys, including *tuj lub, nees zab,* and *tob log;* and rituals and ritual performances such as playing *qeej* at death rites and *hu plig.*

The arts were used to communicate our deepest emotions, which could not be expressed in plain language or in public. They governed our spirits and guided those who had passed on to the spirit world back to our ancestral homeland. They were practical and useful. Because the Hmong did not have a written language until recently, *kwv txhiaj* and knowledge about how to be a *txiv neeb* or *niam neeb* were transmitted verbally from generation to generation.

These time-honored oral traditions are in danger of fading away because of the value Western societies place on the written word over the spoken. When researching Hmong history and culture, Hmong students will often investigate what has been written about the Hmong before or instead of talking to an elder. Rather than taking someone at his or her word, these words must be in writing to be legitimate. Communities or individuals who do not read or write in their own or another language—such as Hmong elders—are perceived as irrelevant or insignificant. Without written text, Hmong voices are overlooked or nonexistent, even in the Asian American studies canon.

A program officer at a foundation once asked me, "How many Hmong writers are there?" I had proposed the development of writing workshops or mentors for Hmong writers, and she wanted to know if there was a critical mass of Hmong writers in Minnesota's Twin Cities. I gave her a numerical count since that was what she wanted to hear, but I should have said, "Just because we aren't as visible as other groups doesn't mean we don't exist." Indeed, it is easy to dismiss a people when they are silent.

Although there were small, local presses, such as *Haiv Hmoob* or *Hmong Forum,* that published Hmong writers, there was not one Hmong voice in any published mainstream Asian or Asian American anthologies in 1994. In the inaugural issue of *Paj Ntaub Voice,* the premier Hmoob literary arts journal I cofounded, I called the Hmong "the undocumented people." I said,

> I hear the Chinese Americans, Japanese Americans, Filipino Americans, Indian Americans, Indonesian Americans, Taiwanese Americans, and Vietnamese Americans speaking. Everyone is speaking about themselves and for themselves— except the Hmong. Where are our voices?

> 'I roam America undocumented . . .' a poet cried in *The Open Boat,* an anthology of poems by Asian Americans, edited by Garrett Hongo. This simple line reminds me of the Hmong in America. At first, it made me sad and then it angered me. Why are we undocumented? Where are the voices of the 27,000 Hmong in St. Paul and Minneapolis? Why are we always waiting for others to tell our stories, to define us, to legitimate us? What are OUR stories? This Hmong silence makes me feel that we have no place in America's history.

It seemed that when we did not know how to tell our own stories in written English, others told them for us. Although many articles and books have been written about the Hmong, most of these do not discuss the artistic life of the Hmong in the United States, instead describing us as simple, preliterate, illiterate, welfare-dependent, and, most recently, violent. Artistic? For non-Hmong, the most artistic items are the colorful costumes that Hmong women wear to New Year celebrations and the storycloths depicting scenes of Hmong crossing the Mekong River or Hmong farm life in Laos. These were the most visible artistic crafts, but they do not represent the artistic soul of the Hmong. As the filmmaker and playwright Va-Megn Thoj has observed, "The storycloths are to Hmong people what teepees are to Native Americans." The identity of a people is reduced to an object that is easily recognized, acceptable, simple, and ancient.

It is essential for the Hmong and other communities of color to express themselves—to write our stories in our own voices and to create our own images of ourselves. When we do not, others write our stories for us, and we are in danger of accepting the images others have painted of us.

How does one encourage an orally based community with no tradition of written literature to develop a written culture? That's exactly the goal of *Paj Ntaub Voice*, the most widely circulated journal in the United States in which readers can find the creative voices of emerging Hmong writers in both Hmong and English.

Paj ntaub (pronounced "pa dao") is the intricate needlework stitched with bright red, orange, green, or purple threads in such styles as batik, cross-stitch, reverse appliqué, or other embroidery forms. *Paj ntaub* is designed to be worn and thus is found on skirts, collars, vests, sashes, purses, hats, and so on. Our name, *Paj Ntaub Voice*, is reflective of our dual identity as

7

Hmong Americans. Our purpose is unprecedented: writing stories with new documentation techniques to reflect the artistic soul of the Hmong community.

Our mission is to provide a community forum to foster Hmong writing and art, thus nurturing the continual growth and celebration of Hmong identity. We aim to build a body of Hmong writers and artists, and in the first eight issues of *Paj Ntaub Voice* we have published Hmong writers from California, District of Columbia, Michigan, Minnesota, New Mexico, North Carolina, and Wisconsin. We promote writing by Hmong writers as well as writing by non-Hmong about the Hmong and the Hmong community. We affirm Hmong writers in a free public reading after each publication, thereby celebrating the writers and their works as well as introducing them to the community.

First housed in Hmong American Partnership (HAP), the only Hmong social service agency with a college student program in 1994, *Paj Ntaub Voice* published its inaugural issue as a twelve-page newsletter. The journal grew to a twenty-five-page publication before joining forces with the Center for Hmong Arts & Talent (CHAT) in 1998. Since joining CHAT, *Paj Ntaub Voice* has matured into a slick eighty-page journal published twice a year and celebrated at two public readings.

Since 1994, *Paj Ntaub Voice* has grown tremendously. Our activities have increased above and beyond the journal; our challenge today is not simply to publish Hmong writers but also to cultivate them. This is a critical time for the Hmong, not only from the perspective of young writers developing their skills but also from the viewpoint of those who look to our elders—the key to our history and culture—who are starting to pass away. The Hmong have been in the United States for over twenty-five years, and there are now Hmong children who speak only English and Hmong elders who speak only Hmong. If nothing is done to capture the *dab neeg,* the life stories and rituals of the Hmong, they will be lost to future generations forever.

In 2001, *Paj Ntaub Voice* left CHAT to become its own entity. Our next stage of development is to continue the journal, cultivate Hmong writers, and collect oral traditions (*dab neeg, kwv txhiaj,* life stories, rituals, and so forth) from the elders. These activities are important because the Hmong are a refugee community trying to remember, establish, develop, and strengthen our own roots in America without compromising our identity.

Providing an overview of Hmong literature is a challenging task. There is no critical mass of creative Hmong writing, which also means there is no available analysis, criticism, or categorization of it. As the writer and artist Bryan Thao Worra stated, "A comprehensive history [of Hmong creative writing] is impossible, really, because it's what I'd classify as orphaned literature. It's there as minute presence, but it's like a ghost that keeps bobbing up to the surface from a deep river. A lot of writers even forget about the things they've written or sent off, or don't even preserve it." My experience working on the journal since 1994 has certainly not made me an expert on the subject. It has, however, given me a starting point for talking about Hmong literature.

To date, literature by and about the Hmong has often fallen into four categories: academic writing, which includes numerous master's theses and doctoral dissertations as well as a plethora of journal articles; third-person narratives, including stories in local and regional newspapers as well as books about the Hmong such as Anne Fadiman's *The Spirit Catches You and You Fall Down;* folktales and folklore such as Norma J. Livo and Dia Cha's *Folkstories of the Hmong,* Charles Johnson and Se Yang's *Myths, Legends, and Folktales from the Hmong of Laos,* and Dr. Lue

Vang's *Grandfather's Path, Grandmother's Way;* and oral histories such as D'Anne Lesch and Jennifer O'Donoghue's *We Are the Freedom People,* Gayle Morrison's *The Sky Is Falling,* and Lillian Faderman's *I Begin My Life All Over.* In addition to these texts in English, there are works by Hmong writers writing in Hmong. Many of these are available at Hmong Arts, Books, and Crafts (ABC), the first Hmong bookstore in the United States, located in St. Paul, Minnesota.

The creative writing published in *Paj Ntaub Voice* is a new category of Hmong literature. Besides the occasional publication of a Hmong writer in newspaper columns, small journals of local organizations, and college campus newsletters or literary arts magazines, *Paj Ntaub Voice* provided a consistent location for people to find creative Hmong writing and for writers to have their work exposed beyond a local setting. There are, however, real challenges in sustaining a Hmoob literary arts journal. To begin with, it is difficult to promote a community journal in a nation where literary arts journals are funded by a limited number of foundations or, more often, ignored. But the journal's advisory board members have struggled with many additional questions. Where are the Hmong writers in a culture that has had no tradition of written literature? How do we encourage those who have been silent to write their stories when they are not used to expressing (and exposing) themselves in written form, in public? How do we nurture emerging writers who are not used to criticism? How do we encourage Hmong writers to write in either Hmong or English when they cannot read or write Hmong and when English is their second language? What is "good" Hmong writing?

The board faces yet another question: How do we encourage a community to appreciate, invest in, and support *Paj Ntaub Voice* by buying the journal or coming to the public readings when they are not accustomed to paying for magazines or attending readings? This is a community that is very private, very protective of its image, and may very well be threatened by the writings of its young people. Once, an older Hmong man called me to ask if I had any morals because we had published a fictional piece about a young Hmong woman who had had multiple sexual partners. He was worried about the image we were portraying to non-Hmong as well as the impact we might have on Hmong youth. I tried explaining the differences between fiction and nonfiction, but I don't think he was satisfied. My own family members have asked me why I publish visual art that they describe as "ugly" or "dirty."

The fact that we are charting new territory does not scare me. As Jeff Yang, the founder of A. *Magazine: Inside Asian America,* stated in *Asian American Dreams,* "We're putting together the pieces, helping to build the foundation of a community and the arts." Yes, we are writing, and we are creating a tradition of written literature as we go along.

The twenty-two Hmong writers in this anthology are a diverse group of individual artists, saying what they need to say. Readers, even Hmong readers, may not always agree with what they write. Most of the writers share the following characteristics:

1. They are emerging.
Some of the writers would disagree with me; others might even be offended by my description of them as "emerging." I can certainly see how they would feel this way. The word may seem condescending because it suggests that a writer will only have "emerged" as a writer if and when s/he has been recognized (legitimized) by someone else: a particular person or persons in the dominant culture. For lack of a better word, however, I use the term "emerging" to signify a lack of publishing experience or history. Most of the writers have not published a novel or a collection of poems, essays, or short stories, nor have they been published in other small or mainstream presses. None

have achieved widespread recognition to the point that they are famous or accepted even in the Hmong community. No one can be considered *the* Hmong or Hmong American writer.

2. They are young.

Some, like myself, were born in Laos, others in the refugee camps in Thailand, and a few in France or America. As the first or first-and-a-half generation to live in the United States, these writers carry the experiences of their parents and grandparents close to their hearts. The ways they remember and tell these stories, however, are their own; theirs is a new way of story-telling. The writers do not claim to speak for or represent Hmong men, Hmong women, Hmong elders, or the Hmong community. They are individual artists, writing about themselves and their experiences.

3. They write in English.

Although Hmong is the mother tongue of the writers, they express themselves in the poetic language they know best—English. Some write in Hmong as well, but it is their works in English that are published here. Frank Chin stated in *The Big Aiiieeeee!*, one of the first anthologies to publish Chinese, Filipino, and Japanese writers, "New experience breeds new history, new art, and new fiction." Writing in English, a "new" language for the Hmong community, is the way these writers tell their stories.

Does this mean they are disconnected from the oral traditions of *dab neeg* and *kwv txhiaj*, which have been the foundation of Hmong literature? Yes, some of them are. For example, I do not know how to sing *kwv txhiaj*. Is it my responsibility to learn? I would argue yes, for I am convinced that the poetry I write in English would be much stronger if I knew how to sing *kwv txhiaj*. I believe that this disconnection from the Hmong oral traditions occurs because the tradition is dying. Elders no longer tell *dab neeg,* and those who know and understand *kwv txhiaj* are mostly adults who sing it once a year at the Hmong New Year celebration.

4. They are from the Midwest.

This anthology is a collection of new works as well as the best works published in *Paj Ntaub Voice* from 1994 to 2001. As such, the authors collected in this anthology are past contributors to *Paj Ntaub Voice*. Most of these contributors are from the Midwest. I believe this is indicative of the work *Paj Ntaub Voice* has done in cultivating, nurturing, and building a body of Hmong writers. It speaks to the presence of *Paj Ntaub Voice* in Minneapolis and St. Paul, Minnesota, which has the greatest concentration of Hmong of any metropolitan region in the world. In addition, Minnesota has a rich tradition of the arts, which has allowed *Paj Ntaub Voice* to flourish. We've received generous grants from foundations including the Asian Pacific Endowment for Community Development (through the St. Paul Foundation), COMPAS: Community Programs in the Arts, the Jerome Foundation, the Metropolitan Regional Arts Council, and the Star Tribune Foundation.

What are these writers writing? They write creative nonfiction, essay, fiction, memoir, drama, and poetry. They write about "Hmong" issues and they write fiction that has nothing to do with the Hmong. They write as the young girl who speaks English to her Hmong-speaking father. They write as the "grizzled face of a boy innocently torn by two cultures." They write as children who remember the traumatic exodus with their families from Laos to Thailand. They write as the daughter of a widow who lost her husband during the Vietnam War and then lost all her possessions as well.

They write about identity within their community, as when Bee Cha muses, "Here in the 'land of opportunity,' to be Hmong is simply *not* enough. We must live beyond ourselves. We have to be different. We *need* to change." And though they love their family and culture, they feel, as Pa Xiong says in "The Green House," that the "traditions have become too heavy / I have worn them on my back for too long . . . / I know I cannot stay / buried voiceless." They write of their new life in America and the realizations that even if they change their hair and eye colors, they will never be white, and that even though they've served in the U.S. Army, one day they'll still be asked to prove they are "American."

They write for those who do not or cannot write their own stories, stories that are as familiar to the culture as the back of one's hands. They write folktales in the tradition in which elders told them, as in Kao Xiong and Dia Cha's "The Lovers: A Halloween Tale of Horror." They also re-imagine the traditional folktales in new ways: Ka Vang's "REM & Dab & Neeg & Dab Neeg" retells the folktale of Yer and the Tiger from the fresh perspective of the tiger/father, while Bryan Thao Worra's story "The True Tale of Yer" tells us that it was actually the hunter who killed the tiger and not the other way around.

They write as the "extraordinary Hmong" who proclaims "this town ain't gonna take me down." With their writings, they piece together "the tangible facts with the imagined facts, hoping to bring my father to life." They write, as Bryan Thao Worra describes, "so people won't forget. / So someone will know. / Lift their broken bodies with my words, bring them out / And say we did not die in vain."

The writings in this anthology cannot be considered social histories of the Hmong. Nor is this anthology a collection of oral histories or *dab neeg* that have been translated from Hmong to English. It is not an overview, "Hmong Life in America 101." Even after reading this anthology, you will have gained only one glimpse of a slice of Hmong life in America. Like *Paj Ntaub Voice*, these writings mark the foundation of written Hmong literature as works of art first and foremost and then perhaps as socio-

logical or anthropological findings. Along with *Paj Ntaub Voice,*
Bamboo Among the Oaks is the beginning of a Hmong American
literature and a literate Hmong American community. It is the
first anthology of Hmong American writers to be distributed
nationwide.

It is an exciting time to be Hmong in America. The writings
collected in *Paj Ntaub Voice* and in *Bamboo Among the Oaks* docu-
ment our experiences here. We have written and are writing
our own stories. "My voice has come out at last! It is like a raging storm waiting to shower itself over the world," proclaims
May Lee in "The Voice." Although the Hmong have not had a
tradition of written literature, we are building one. We are the
creators of our own history from this point on.

MAI NENG MOUA

Recovering to the Hills

Excerpt from Memoirs of a Lap Dog, *a novel in progress.*

It was a hot July fourth at McMurray Park, where thousands of Hmong were showcasing their athletic abilities. I watched from a hill as the traffic of Hmong moved in the valley, which had become an arena for soccer, volleyball, and kato. There was a small breeze blowing, sending smells of hot papaya salad, barbecued chicken, grilled sausage, grilled fish, and *kaub poob* to my nostrils. I sat there, watching the Hmong below moving about like black ants. I thought about who I was and why I didn't seem to be a part of this unique culture whose history was as old as China. I watched Hmong women walk among the masses and saw their beauty. But I found myself unhappy, unclear as to why I didn't belong on this hill. I started walking back to my apartment, which was just around the corner and under the railroad bridge.

I found a path suited for my own two feet through the maze of Hmong and debris. My eyes focused on not stepping into the discarded papaya salad on the ground and did not see the ocean of Hmong women in their summer outfits. Short brunettes in platform shoes, tight flared pants, and tiny T-shirts that had Chinese calligraphy on them. Short brunettes with eyebrows plucked to nothing and replaced with fake brows drawn in with dark eyeliner. I did not see the blonde, blue-eyed women who had always appealed to my senses or the black beauties who could send me to cloud nine and steal a moment or two of my life. I wondered why the group of Hmong men ahead was making such a commotion as to which chick they would like to get digits from. The men were in suits and ties in the middle of a sports tournament, all dressed like they were going to the prom. I started to laugh.

An unfamiliar figure blurred past me, but the distinctive blonde hair made her stand out. I had to turn my head to get a better glimpse of this yellow rose in a poppy field, but it turned out to be just yellow petals, unlike a certain country daisy years ago. I could still remember her tall, tan, slim figure contrasting with my short, petite, egg-white sister as we watched the U.S. national men's volleyball team play against Greece. But as I look back on our relationship, the movie *Breakfast at Tiffany's* sums it all up, and ironically a bit of that movie was in *Dragon: The Bruce Lee Story*, the last movie we saw together.

Life is a maze of abysses that you jump into one after another or maybe it just seems that way to me, but I still think about her once in a while. Speaking of mazes, this earth-beaten path to my place seems like one, only the tall hedges have been replaced by rattan grass. How can I find my way out of this woven *vaab*, where the good rice kernels are being sifted? I must be one of those lucky black ones you find lingering at the bottom. Maybe that is why at my cousin's wedding I got "jungle fever." Out of all the ladies there, she was the most breathtaking, this dark-skinned beauty with the most beautiful black opal eyes I had ever seen. Maybe because she was the only rare pearl there, that was why I had learned to love her most. But like rare gems, she slipped away or maybe I didn't know how to appreciate her as much as I thought I did. I guess there is still hope, or have I become too saturated from my non-Hmong encounters?

I laughed that I, a Hmong man, could not appreciate these short brunettes with their round porcelain faces. I thought that maybe I was gay when it came to Hmong women or perhaps I had a phobia of some sort. Whatever the case may be, I found them to be trashy, like the garbage floating around the tournament. As I made my way out of the park and back into my apartment, I started to think about why I felt this way when it came to Hmong, relationships, and love.

I thought, who could this one person be, my Hmong lady? Images of my sisters, aunts, cousins, and nieces began to appear like the slide shows I had learned to tolerate in art history classes. But the image of Botticelli's *Venus* rising on a seashell and about to be draped by a red, blue, and green *paj ntaub* instead of a purple robe remained in my head. Even E. H. Gombrich's quote on the painting rang true:

> Botticelli's *Venus* is so beautiful that we do not notice the unnatural length of her neck, the steep fall of her shoulders and the queer way her left arm is hinged to the body. Or, rather, we should say that these liberties which Botticelli took with nature in order to achieve a graceful outline add to the beauty and harmony of the design because they enhance the impression of an infinitely tender and delicate being, wafted to our shores as a gift from heaven.

Kuv lub meej mom nrhav tau tawm kuv lub plawv qhuab qha rua kuv tas kuv lub neej puv dlhau hwv lawm vim has tas kuv yog memkuj. How does someone like me return home? It has been twenty-two years since I last played among the rice fields. I am a long way from home.

I thought back to a couple of years ago when I was in Japan, in search of an identity. I was in love with a brunette with the face of a deity. Yet I was not happy, because my parents could never agree to our wedding nor to the fact that I would be in Japan for most of my life. But this was the only time I had ever been close to loving a girl who was similar to me. Faced with cultural differences and language barriers, I tried to live among the Japanese. I worked hard at becoming who I would never be. But in the end, we departed to our corners of the world.

I was alone in my apartment, trying to recover something I had lost long ago—my identity, my being. As the dark night lit up with fireworks celebrating the independence of this nation, I tried to relinquish my own sadness at being an individual.

What have you become, Kaub Yaaj? Aahh! Oh where, oh where can she be, the Hmong girl who would liberate me from my confusion? Are you out there? Are you among the rice fields, in the hills? Have I lost my chance to recover what I had lost for so long? I screamed at myself, thinking of my Hmong Venus.

While I sat there, the phone rang. It was a good Hmong friend of mine. He said that he had just met the Hmong woman of his dreams. I was happy for him because he, like me, had never found Hmong women appealing. I spent the night with Jack Daniel's, and we talked about the moments that had shaped my existence. I was in good company.

I woke up around noon the next day with a headache and a dry throat. I took a shot of water to quench my thirst, and then the doorbell rang. It was my buddies from Kansas. They were visiting for the tournament and wanted to take me out for some dim sum. It was the beginning of a good day.

The subject at the table was the hoochies they had met while up here. They recalled the ones with big boobs, platforms, and black lipstick. I chuckled. They talked about how it was getting worse now that they are older. Finding Hmong women their age was hard, and the ones they did meet were divorced. I chuckled. I was ten years older than they were, and I felt out of place. I was a bad example for them: locked in a cage with my identity and unable to break free from the bonds that tied me. In search of tomorrow, in search of a better paradise, in search of my mystery, in search of a Hmong woman who would set me free.

They asked me when I was going to get married. I said when their kids were their age. We laughed together. But inside I was afraid that I could never go back to the hills. Each day I thought about her—the Hmong woman who would help me go back to the hills and harvest the rice that had been planted. I thought about it all the time. Who was she?

I thought back on my life. There have been only four Hmong women in it. My first female Hmong friend is now married and

lives in Denver with her husband of three years. My first love
has been buried in Denver for three years. My shrink, who is
in love with my friend, is now in contact with me after a three-
year hiatus. Finally, my best and beloved Hmong goddess shares
her life with me but we see things differently.

One of my friends asked me what I was thinking about.
I said that I was just thinking that I'd rather be fishing for blue
marlins. He asked me why. I said that I believed I had met my
Hmong woman yesterday but that I just didn't know how to let
her in. He said we all met our Hmong women yesterday, but for
some reason they didn't meet us. I told him that everyone had
a hill to return to, and I wished that we had one, too.

My friend said it was okay: "We will always have bilingual
Hmong girls to laugh with, drink tea with, eat sushi with, and
speak broken Hmong with. But the irony is that each of us will
never recover to the hills because we can't stand on our own
two feet on such slanted terrain. We need someone else to balance with."

We laughed hard, then smiled and drank our tea.

I know that I will never truly find what I am looking for,
as long as I don't know what exactly it is that I am seeking. But
for now I am happy. At least I am thinking about returning to
the hills.

Bee Cha ⚜

Being Hmong Is Not Enough

If birds are dreams of the Hmong, then a flightless fowl has to be our worst nightmare. Then again, we seem pretty content just being chickens and cocks in our own sheltered pen. Have our minds become domesticated? Have our dreams repatriated? Have our souls become entangled by these colorful threads of customs?
From a journal entry written upon returning
to St. Paul, Minnesota, for a visit

It's been nearly six years since these unsettling questions forced me to take a sabbatical leave from my family and the Hmong community altogether to explore the issue of *what I am* in the shadow of *who I am*. To further search for answers to the question of where the "I" in Hmong is, I deliberately locked myself up in the basement of my loneliness until I was enlightened. Once in a while, I find it essential to resist social and cultural norms in order to achieve a sense of personal identity outside of and apart from the community. Unfortunately, this time higher education, maturity, and isolation have only bred more cynicism, skepticism, criticism, and a relentless fury about being Hmong. But because I genuinely believe that negativity is a catalyst for change, I consider these revelations to be the "bitter fruits of novelty," which, if digested thoughtfully, will lead to profound implications. At last, antipathy has given me the audacity to reason without fear and speak without remorse. During my peaceful isolation, I have had opportunities to contemplate numerous repressed thoughts such as "Gentrified Mind," "Living Lavish, Eating Ramen," "The Hmong Misology," "*Hmong:* The Unnecessary Adjective," and "Thoughtful Defiance," as well as the following significant topics.

The Theory of Necessary Return
Eight years ago, I wrote a parable entitled "One Step Behind a Bird," in which I portrayed the helplessness of being caught in this first-generation, bicultural phenomenon. The story ends

with a bald eagle (personifying the American dream) tempting a Hmong man to completely abandon the values of *who he is* and plunge himself into the depths of uncertainty in order to be transformed into a bird of flight. The inconclusive ending of the tale seems to be a parallel experience for many of us. Sooner or later, each of us will face the same dilemma as we are forced to make a decision between what we want and what we need to do with our lives as first-generation Hmong Americans.

Upon graduation from my master's program, I wanted to travel to Europe and live out my childhood dream of becoming a successful international architect. But as a responsible Hmong son, I could not wander far from my ailing parents, who had risked everything after the war to ensure my well-being in America. My parents needed me to stay close to take care of them and secure the future of our family and clan. When I decided not to act on the selfish impulse to travel to Europe, I thought it was a courageous sacrifice. Believing that no one from an American school would be accepted to work for a prestigious firm abroad, I was content to stay here. However, I was devastated when I heard that a graduate from my school was offered employment at Foster and Partners, an international award–winning architecture firm in London that I had wanted to work for as a young designer. With my talents, experience, and confidence, even God could not dispute my qualifications. But I was *hmong*. I was cursed. It was as if I was held, tied, and pulled back by these ancient "threads of customs." For someone who believes in the might of the Individual, I reluctantly acknowledged the existence of a greater force at work. Restless and undeterred, I wanted to find answers—even if I had to make them up—to explain why everyone, including myself, has to return home. Ultimately, frustration, resentment, and the need to move beyond self-pity culminated in the formulation of a theory explaining this appalling tendency that continues to pull us back home.

The Theory of Necessary Return stems from the moral certainty that, because of cultural and/or personal needs that must first be obliged, all (especially the first) bicultural generations are deterred from indulging in a complete and autonomous exploration of their free will. Through time, this restraint becomes conditionally understood that *what we are* (i.e., our will to succeed) cannot free us from *who we are* (the obligations of being Hmong). Essentially, because needs take precedence over wants, we cannot pursue the "American dream" and simultaneously neglect the Hmong culture without grave consequences. In the end, it becomes necessary to return home and attend to the immediate needs rather than face the uncertain price of wanting something different.

To better understand the cause of this familiar retrogression, our needs must be sorted into two distinct categories: consequential needs and self-inflicted needs.

I. Consequential Needs

Moral Obligations: Human beings are instinctively altruistic, especially when it involves family members. "My parents risked their lives to make sure I live today. They are illiterate and now very old; I need to take care of them."

Cultural Obligations: Some Hmong have inherited cultural responsibilities that cannot be easily neglected. "I am next in line for clan leadership. I have no way out but to act my role. I need to be responsible!"

Social Obligations: With more and more Hmong seeking higher education, many feel that it is necessary to apply their knowledge where it is most needed. "With my expertise, I need to start an organization to help the Hmong become socially and financially viable."

II. Self-Inflicted Needs

Contentment: When we become too complacent, the greatest danger is that we will do nothing else to encourage the progression of the Hmong. "I am comfortable with the community as it is; I see no reason to change anything."

Insecurity: Being fearful of uncertainty, we will always remain victims of circumstance. "I need to be close to my family, friends, and lovers; therefore I cannot and will not leave the community."

Irresponsibility: Too often we have seen today's youth (and even adults) turning to gangs or mischievous activities only to crawl back home for full parental support once their youthful zeal has expired. "I don't give a fuck about school or jobs; I need to have fun while I'm still young."

Distinguishing between consequential and self-inflicted needs helps us to understand the two forces (cultural suppression and personal repression) that are responsible for our hardship and indecision. While one holds us back, the other keeps us down. When we allow the two forces to conspire, there is little hope for independence (or sanity) because of the tremendous fear of being banished by our own people. In due course—despite what you are, when you leave, where you have been, or how long you have been away—you will return to the community.

This notion of return is not, however, always a literal translation of "going back home." Too often it's a mental reversion to that common hmong aura, typically characterized by our traditional beliefs, excessive behaviors, and corrupt ethics. We should recognize that our relapse has detrimental repercussions on the Hmong, both socially and individually. It ubiquitously contributes to the phenomenon that I have referred to as "a bowl of sticky rice," where we naturally clump back together, not wanting to go beyond the boundary of our community even when opportunities present themselves. We simply resort to the convenience of "just being hmong," as if ignorant or apathetic toward this disease of "learned helplessness." Needless to say, this bowl of rice has turned foul, producing a sheltered ethnocentric pride, fostering our inferiority complex and our hatred, distrust, and fear of and prejudice toward others around us.

What It Means to Be Hmong

It is disturbingly ironic that although *Hmong* means "free" the majority of us feel just the opposite, "trapped." How, then, can we be Hmong? The truth is, how we lived in China, Laos, and Thailand cannot explain what we feel or justify who we are today in America. This discrepancy clearly confirms that we must redefine *Hmong* in the context of our contemporary issues. Even though the essence of who we are (what *Hmong* is) has changed very little, the implication of *Hmong* (what it means) has dramatically evolved. Since we have been known historically as nomads, it would only seem appropriate that "who we are" is determined by the places and events that we experience along the way. With the Return's traumatic impact we cannot (and should not) refute description of this period as another turning point in Hmong history. Hence, the following can be extrapolated:

Time/Event	Implication
Pre-Laos–1975	
(through the Vietnam War)	*Hmong* means *Free*
1975–1990 (post–Vietnam War)	*Hmong* means *Surviving*
1990–present (assimilation in the United States)	*Hmong* means *????*

If I were an optimist, I would concur that during the current epoch, the Hmong are actually "thriving." Due to our exceptional adaptation to this fast-paced econo-technological world, we have flourished despite enormous barriers. This is true, however, only within the micro context of refugee communities. Moreover, our community may have flourished socially and economically, but in terms of mental progress—the way we think—little has changed. For centuries, the Hmong have resisted change and refused interactions with non-Hmong in order to maintain ethnic purity, but now that time and place have changed drastically we can no longer ignore the outcomes of such senseless resistance. Here in the context of America, the mentality of this first generation has naturally digressed from the accepted norm due to the mounting pressures of individual rights and unrestricted freedom. Momentarily, we stand right in the middle of this shambled confusion where the notion of being born Hmong and raised American has made it extremely troublesome for us to know (or even accept) who we are anymore. Unfortunately, as if out of retribution, the Theory of Necessary Return makes certain that the less we know what Hmong is, the more we must know what it means: To be Hmong means our education must take a back seat to our Tradition. It means our Culture will not permit new knowledge to adulterate its old Customs. To be Hmong means it is more important to have a face than an ego. It means we suffer quietly under the pretense of Hmong pride despite the agony of victimization. To be Hmong means not wanting less and not needing more. It means we prefer that convenience establish standards for us. To be Hmong means the concept "I" does not exist. It means all our decisions need validation from the elders. To be Hmong means women must return to serve the men and men the Tradition. It means that the American dream can be a Hmong's worst nightmare.

Now the term Hmong suddenly encompasses a more complex layer of meanings, indicative of both our state of being and our mentality. To be *Hmong* means:

1) to be free,
2) to be a survivor,

3) to be content, or

4) to be trapped.

The first few steps in the evolution of progress require that we be able to answer our own questions, making this extended definition, in the context of our struggle, a quintessential discovery that allows us to better understand ourselves as Hmong in America. The next time we are asked, "What does it mean to be Hmong, now and then?" our replies will be nothing short of concise.

The Concept of "Absolute Hmonglessness"

One of my recent aphorisms says that "when it comes to progress, there is no crime greater than not wanting and no action worse than just waiting." Regrettably, we have accomplished both, and, not surprisingly, we have achieved nothing. Those who are noble enough to recognize the need for social development have only fallen into the trap of trying to change the world without first changing themselves, while those who are apathetic about the issues have either segregated themselves from the rest of the community or remained submissive and passive in order to avert the complications imposed by the soul-constricting traditions. And it seems that being hmong has become an inevitable obsession that offers little hope that the situation will change. I fear perhaps even more than I believe that we are so overwhelmed with who we are that we forget to realize where we are and what we could become.

For those of my generation, it appears that becoming a typical hmong has developed into a careless and casual routine. And whether we are conscious of it or not, we cannot ignore the overall effects on the Hmong community as a result of this mental reversion. Our bigotry, silence, apathy, indifference, contentment, ignorance, dishonesty, and lack of professionalism (or class) will force us to remain synonymous with mediocrity and shame. Then even this so-called higher education won't be able to provide ethnic redemption or personal exemption from this social disgrace due to our inflated emphasis on looking good rather than being the best. Knowing that with a B.A. one is lionized, with an M.A. one could be glorified, and with a Ph.D. one would be deified, many have tossed their minds onto this shelf of convenience in search of a pretentious spot along the community wall to showcase their (often exaggerated) merits. Tragically, living in America has unquestionably exacerbated our greed for materialistic wealth and unnecessary social status. These are sad consequences because the Hmong way of life used to be simple; now the fad is to conspicuously display more wealth and power than we are worth and willing to stand for, respectively. As a matter of fact, I fervently believe that we have become more morally corrupted. I can't understand, for instance, why the celebration of our culture cannot exist without the desire to profit from the community and exploit young girls through the so-called beauty contest. And expressed in my ten-year absence from the annual Hmong New Year is my contempt for the decline of our cultural mentality. Over a decade ago I wrote in my journal that "if we are growing [mentally], then we are changing; but if we are just changing [materialistically], then we have not grown at all." Today, I am still not surprised by the irony that although we have changed much materialistically, mentally we haven't changed at all.

As we enter a new millennium, I wonder what it will take for us to realize and accept that change isn't progress if it's not thoughtful. I speculate with great anxiety simply because there aren't too many genuinely thoughtful Hmong out there. Is this a gloomy omen for the future of the Hmong? Many will not care, but I see introspection as an integral part of change since it represents a mental process of freeing ourselves from who we are so that we can achieve a sense of sacred awareness of our selves and our environment. Sitting here alone at night writing this essay, I can only wonder with sadness: Who will stand by my side when I choose to fight for the preservation of the rain forest or who will even pitch in a dime when I collect donations to help save the humpback whales from extinction? It's no excuse that being Hmong should preclude us from being concerned about worldly issues. But if we are apathetic about the growing landfills or the depleting ozone layer, will we at least take notice of the outstanding issues at home? When will we allow our mothers, wives, sisters, and aunts to sit among us at the clan-gathering dinner table? And when will we stop selling our daughters in marriage at such a steep bride price to exhibit the social status of the clan? What Hmong organization will stand up to make a pledge to look for ways to help control the population explosion within our community? Which clan leader will no longer force a fourteen-year-old to marry her rapist in order to save the family from disgrace? When will we find just one precious moment late at night to open our eyes to these issues and then sigh deeply before going to sleep?

I must confess that having an open mind for change can be as frustrating as it is lonely. Fortunately, we will never feel lonesome if we make efforts to be in tune with our thoughts. And I believe that when we are able to feast on these "bitter fruits" alone, we will realize that the less we think like hmong, the better Hmong person we will become. This understanding is what I have identified as the concept of "absolute hmonglessness." The idea is not unlike the mathematic principle of absolute value. From high school algebra we learned, for example, that the absolute value of the number -4 is 4. Similarly, if the absolute value of a negative thought is still a thought, then the absolute value of "hmonglessness" is just "hmong." This undemanding logic reveals that we cannot further demean ourselves despite what we think of the Hmong. Regardless of what we think, when we strip away the attitude of our emotion, we are left with just the magnitude of that emotion. And through the power of introspection, the attitude "I hate the Hmong" can be transformed into "I am passionate about the Hmong."

Realize that the key to understanding this "absolute" principle has little to do with how we feel and more with how we can use it to advance our thinking. In fact, I believe that the more we dislike who we are, the sooner we realize that the only way to prevail over our social stagnation and ethnic stigma is to become a much more distinguished Hmong. At the end of the day, we can use the effect of this theory to help us make a distinction between just *being Hmong* (the nature of who we are) and obsessively *becoming hmong* (the mentality of who we were). This is a significant development in understanding where we are in the spectrum of mental progression because it ensures, at last, that we don't have to be hmong to remain Hmong anymore. Since time and place have changed, these two Hmong-defining elements have become mutually exclusive of each other and, therefore, changing one cannot affect the other. Quite frankly, I wouldn't be a designer (the symbol of what I am) if I had to become hmong first. And being what I am does not, by any means, dilute who I am. I like to think that it helps to make me a better person. And, ironically, despite this mentality, I will still be remembered by the community as a Hmong architect.

Change requires a private consideration because the implication of Hmong, whether for the better or for the worse, is only the beginning. It shouldn't be a revelation to understand that changing the mind is much easier than trying to change the Hmong. And until we demand a better personal response to this hampered notion of *what it means to be Hmong,* our lives will miserably remain the same. I, too, have fallen ill of hearing, "Why do the Hmong do this?" When will they ask, "How do the Hmong do that?" I think we have become so comfortably hmong that we've lost the fuel of resentment that would encourage us to act responsively. Without the anger of being victims and the knowledge of our subdued situation we will have no validation to serve our purposes and no vision to guide our paths toward a better Hmong life. What use is a feminist movement without the anguish? What worth is this expensive liberal schooling without personal applications? What pride is there in being Hmong if we don't take part in re-shaping our diminished cultural mentality? Only a fool would subscribe to the naïve notion that if we know too much and speak too loud we may no longer be Hmong. Rest assured: whether or not we give a damn about these Hmong issues, the Theory of Necessary Return will certainly remind us of *who* we are. We may bitch all day long about the distress of being Hmong, but at the end of the day we will always return home to a bowl of warm rice and chicken soup flavored with fresh blades of lemon grass picked from our humble backyard garden.

My intention in crafting this essay—quoted and reconstructed from actual journal entries—is far from trying to persuade the community to think differently. Instead, I want to expose and explore these issues as a concerned Hmong. And I won't apologize for not obscuring these pungent emotions behind the indirectness of poetry. It is my belief that if we are to become sensible Hmong persons, we have to be sincere with ourselves and be up front about the issues occurring in the community. Hence, the content of this essay is meant to reflect the passion of my thoughts as genuinely expressed in my diary. However, by my own default I am aware that many Hmong will despise my arrogance and perhaps even more will loathe my integrity, because now I have allowed honesty to sew an ugly storycloth of these esoteric issues. Truthfully, the negative reception that I will receive for my sincerity is the least of my worries. The moment we no longer fear the worst is the day we are prepared for something better. When that time comes I hope I don't have to stand alone. And no one should have to feel lonely as long as we all believe that although we cannot escape the gravitational pull of the Return theory, we must return a different and better Hmong person. The future of the Hmong should be what we are trying to create and not just what we are trying to preserve. Having said that, we need to rethink the notion of *who we are* in light of *what we are,* and not the other way around. Sadly, if we don't,

> no bird feathers will grow and no mountain man will fly if he doesn't accept Prometheus' torch [to burn away the unnecessary threads that have entangled our freedom]. There is no denying that being Hmong has an unforgiving price when you don't want to be just content. Here in the "land of opportunity," to be Hmong is simply *not* enough. We must live beyond ourselves. We have to be different. We *need* to change. Bigotry does not amend our thoughts; apathy cannot reprieve our sufferings; silence will not remunerate our struggles. And I, for one, can no longer be content in holding back.

A Good Hmong Woman

Transcriber's Introduction *This is an excerpt from my interviews with my mother, taped in 1995. Names, including my own, have been changed to protect the identities of all involved. As Hmong custom dictated, my mother left her family and lived with my father's family when she married him. This tradition is sometimes traumatizing for Hmong women because they have to leave behind everything—their families, their God, their connections, their work, and so forth—and adopt the ways of their new families. However, not all experiences of daughters-in-law are as dramatic as the one described here.*

I. On Being a Daughter-in-Law

I was eighteen when I married. We had no place of our own. When I came to live with your father, we lived with your grandmother and grandfather. When your father went away to be a soldier, I went with him to live at the military base for a year and then when I had [your older brother] Bee, I came back to live with Grandmother and Grandfather.

When your father came home, your grandparents did one thing. They pretended to love me, but when your father went away they did another thing. Whenever their son came back, they'd ask for my opinion. When they cooked, they'd ask me, "Daughter-in-law, how should we cook these vegetables?" They did that so that their son would not know. So he would think, "Oh, even though I am away, my mom and my wife know how to love each other."

There was one time when I brought home cucumbers [from the farm]. Grandmother wouldn't let your uncles eat them. "If you don't eat those cucumbers, will you die? If you can't live without them then eat them," she said.

Your father said, "Eat them. Why shouldn't you eat them? We brought them here for everybody to eat."

Grandmother said, "Son, you are not a man. An evil person like that, you must hit her. You should hit her."

That Grandmother, she's very clever. She said really nice words but her heart was on the side of her buttocks. When your father was near, she smiled while she talked sweet words to me, but when he was not around . . . When I cooked, she did not want to eat with me. She was afraid that I wouldn't know that she didn't like me, so she said to her daughters, "Mai and Der, pack one spoon for you, one for me, one for your father, and another for your brother." She said this. What about me? They didn't count me as part of the family. At first, I went with them to the farm, but later I did not. I thought, "Forget it. I am not even part of the family." Even if I farmed with them a whole day, they didn't care, so I didn't go. I stayed home and shelled the rice [for the family], but when they got home, they shelled their own rice and put it in another basket.

I don't know why Grandmother hated me. When she talked to other people, she said she was the good one and I was the evil one—the one that was wrong—but I didn't see what I did wrong. They never said, "Daughter-in-law, you did not do this well. You did this wrong," so I didn't know. But they kept telling other people that I was the wrong one—one hundred percent wrong. They kept "shooting" at me. They said it was my fault, but no one sat down and fixed things. We got mad through our eyes and our hearts.

Grandfather was the same, too. Whatever Grandmother did, he did, too. Once, our sows had babies, and they only castrated their piglets. Three mornings after the piglet is born, you have to castrate them. You cut away the balls so the piglet will grow big and fat. I was so mad. I had to castrate my own piglet. Bee held the legs, and I did it. I knew how to do it already because when I was little I used to catch all the piglets for my father. I would hold the legs, and he would cut the balls.

Whatever was mine—if I put my sugarcane down over here or there—none of them would eat it. Whenever someone touched it, Grandmother would say, "Don't touch that. It belongs to Bee's mother. It's theirs." Theirs? "Theirs" is the people on the outside. I am on the inside: why say "they"? At first, I was *tu siab* and I cried, but later I didn't cry anymore. I didn't care.

I thought, "I am their daughter-in-law. They married me, and I came to live with them. Why don't they don't know how to use my strength? How could a grandmother be so stupid? I bring home a pile of cucumbers, and I never said, 'Don't ever touch my cucumbers.' She is the grandmother; she holds all the power in her hands; why does she tell the younger ones not to eat them?" I never told any of them not to eat it, so I decided that if they wanted to eat it, it was there. If they didn't, it was not going to bite anyone.

Grandmother trained her two younger daughters-in-law to treat me the same.

"You two, that Hmong woman is mean. It is hers; don't touch it," she would tell them. She would not eat whatever I brought home. She would rather go and borrow it from the neighbors and tell them that I wouldn't let her have any. That person then would hate me, too. She'd say, "Why is your daughter-in-law so evil? I just saw her bring some home." Later, that same person would ask me, "Why didn't you give any vegetables to your family to eat?" Only then would I know what Grandmother had done.

II. On Being Heavy-Hearted

Our family had many problems. I was their daughter-in-law, and I came up against a lot of problems. If I pooped, I was wrong. If I farted, I was wrong. If I coughed, I was wrong. Imagine a little child walking on a line. If your toe steps over the line on this side, you get hit. If your toe steps over the line on that side, you get hit. I was so mad.

There was nothing to clear my heart. I couldn't do anything. I could've gone and told someone, but they would have said,

"We've never hit her. We've never yelled at her. She's bad. We're good. We would never do these things." They hated me [then], but not as much as when my second son died. At that time, your father was the one who hated me most. The number-one person who hated me. His face was always dark. Grandmother was always telling him things.

Once, when I went to fetch some water and they thought I hadn't returned yet, I was outside [and] I heard the whole family say to your father, "A wife like yours, you should just kick her. Send her to the hospital."

"Kick her so hard her veins will wrap around your toes."

"Make her shit in her pants."

"You're not a man. That's why your wife is like that."

"Your wife is this bad. She does this and this."

I was out there for half an hour listening to them, and then I came inside. I said to them, "My husband and I do not know how to argue and hit each other. Our life is like an oven; you don't feed it so it lives. You poke at it so it dies. If someday your son hits me or slaps me, I will get all of you. If my mother and father told me to do evil things to you, to not listen to you, you would be upset, too. I came to live with you and your son. I was not lazy. If I was, I have relatives: why don't you take me to them? Why do you keep telling your son to kick me? I am upset with all of you. Remember what I have told you. If and when your son lifts his hand to hit me, I will get all of you." I said, "I am here. If you want to kick me, go ahead," and they all ran away and didn't answer me.

I said, "I am telling you, Husband, if you ever hit me, I will get your whole family. I want to die. Do you all want to die with me? I am so mad. I came to live with you, and you didn't love me. Now I know it's because your family tells you not to."

That was our big fight, but it wasn't the biggest one. There was another time. Your uncle had gone fishing and had caught a big fish. He wanted to take it to the market to sell it, but I said, "Well, we don't have anything for breakfast so why don't you give it to me, and I'll cook it for breakfast." They hated me so much already I should've let him sell it, but I took it and cooked it for breakfast instead. All the men ate first. There was only Cousin-Grandmother Tou Lor, your father, and I left. The fish was on a stick, and your father took it and put it in front of him, between his legs. I was on his right and Grandmother Tou Lor sat opposite of him.

Your father said to me, "Why don't you eat it? You're so bossy."

Grandmother Tou Lor said, "I want to but it's in front of you."

I said, "If you want people to eat it, put it on the table. You don't want to let other people have it." I said this because it wasn't just him and me eating; there was another woman at the table. I couldn't just reach over and pick at it. It would have been awkward for the other woman.

But your father said, "Did I put it right in my lap?!"

He was acting like a monkey, so I said, "Oh, my goodness. Why are you acting like a monkey?" He got mad at these words. He said I'd called him a monkey.

Then he said, "You evil lady. You bad wife. You dead face." He threw his spoon on the table, spilling rice everywhere.

"Don't you know we hate you so much? What do we have to do to kill you? You barren sow who does not know how to cry. You visitor who does not know how to go home. We hate you so much, but you don't know. If the barren sow knew how to cry and the visitor knew how to return home, then you would know we hated you. We hate you."

At that time, it seemed like a rock came up and blocked my throat. I couldn't breathe. I couldn't even cry. I couldn't say a thing. It was too painful. I couldn't eat. I dropped my spoon and ran into the bedroom to grab Bee, my *paj ntaub* basket, and my umbrella. It was raining hard; it was the seventh month, [the] month of the monsoons. I went outside and decided that I was going to my mother's house. I went to a spare house nearby for five minutes, and then I returned to the house. There was a man in our house who was related to my mother. He just happened to visit when your father yelled at me, so I thought, "I will go back and talk to him."

I said to him, "Good or bad, you were here when my husband yelled at me. These words I will tell my relatives. You have heard his words to me. Someday, if my lungs still have fat or my heart has blood, I will tell my relatives. I want you to help me remember these words you heard today."

He said, "These words are not words you use to discipline someone. I will be your witness."

Then I went to my mother's. I got there, and I thought, "The whole family will get together and yell at me." I didn't tell my mother what had happened. I just got up and said, "I have to go back, Mom." I came back and hid in the garden outside the house. They were all yelling at me. Saying all sorts of things—everything. Toward the evening, your father came out, and I was afraid of being seen so I ran inside.

Everyone said, "Oh, she's back!"

I said, "You want to kick me? I am here. They say if the younger one can't do it, the older one should. I am here. Come hit me." They all ran away, so I was the only one left in the house.

Then they called all their relatives to come and yell at me. They told me I shouldn't go to my relatives. They would lose money, a lot of money. Your father promised he would buy a pig to heal my spirit and love me the same again. We all yelled at each other until evening, so I said, "Fine, if you don't want me to tell my relatives, I won't." I said that, but my heart was so sad.

Ever since then my heart changed a lot. I knew they didn't love me, so I didn't want to do anything anymore. There was no longer that desire to do things to the best of my abilities. I lived mediocrely. I just lived with your father, but there was not that feeling of missing him. Even if your father did not come home from the military base, I lived like I do now [without him]. If he did come home, I still lived like I do now. After we had those talks, your father calmed down a little bit. He stopped putting his gun to my head. He had done it three times before. He never hit me because he went to the monks and they told him, "Your wife does not want to live with you. She does not want you. Your wife, you cannot hit her. If she does not leave you, she will kill herself. She is very angry with you because you do not love her," so he was afraid of this.

The only time your father loved me was after I had [your younger brother] Ger. Everyone saw it. They all said, "Oh, now that Aunt had a baby boy, Chong loves her more." Everyone saw that he didn't love me before. If your husband does not find you worthy, everyone else will hate you just as much. They don't even want to look at you. I saw that he didn't love me before, but I couldn't do anything about it.

I told your father I forgave him, but my heart could not forgive him. Even when he went and talked to his girlfriends, I didn't care. I didn't want to live with him anymore. I didn't have anything in my heart for him. Grandmother would yell at me, but I didn't care. If they didn't want to eat my food, as long as I didn't hide it in the bedroom, I didn't care. If they didn't eat it, so what? I could feed it to my pigs later. At least they'll remember that their master was good and fed them well. At least they won't bite.

When your father died, they hated me even more. They even hated you children. They were only nice to me when your father was alive because they needed him—needed his money to spend. They had to be nice to me. Your father, he never bought me anything. He was the oldest, and so he gave all his money to the family. Your uncle was in school, so your father's monthly money went to him. Whatever was left was for the family. After your father died, there was no place to eat and drink, so they hated us. They didn't even feed you guys.

One time, [when] you and I went to the farm, the family did an *ua neeb kho* ritual. When we came back home, they wouldn't let us into the house. There was a branch outside the door, preventing people on the outside from entering. We were in the house for eight months, and they didn't do it. When we went to the farm for two days, they did it. They didn't tell us. We came back, and they just didn't let us go into the house. Ger came out to see us, and they came out and beat him. We begged for some cornstarch. I told Bee to ask Grandmother for some, but one of your uncles said, "Even if I had it, I wouldn't give it to you. I'd rather throw it away in the valley and see what noise it makes." Bee brought us three little sticks of rice, and we went to eat it at my mother's house. The next day, we went to dig yams, and that's how we were able to survive.

When we were away at the farm, Grandfather went through our stuff and claimed whatever was your father's as his own and took it to his bedroom. All our sacks were empty. One of the girls told me it was Grandfather who took it.

After your father died, I had one sow left. This was all I had left of my life with your father. I told a cousin-grandmother that I wanted to take the sow to the market and sell it. She told Grandmother and Grandfather, who were hiding in the jungle. The next morning, at seven, they all came back and started cleaning the pots and pans and putting them on the stove. I asked them why they were doing this, but the two younger daughters-in-law didn't even tell me. They said Grandmother told them to do it. I waited to see what they were doing. After the water boiled, they went and got my sow and killed her. They didn't even say a word to me such as, "Chong and you have worked hard. This is your only sow left. We are hungry.

Can we kill it for everyone?" They just killed her. One of the daughters-in-law had the guts to go and cut a whole leg for her relatives. I was so mad. I went and cut the other leg, too.

I said, "After my husband died, all I have is this sow. I'm going to cut this leg for my mother."

And then when we fried the fat, that younger daughter-in-law said, "I'm going to take some to my mother."

And I said, "Me, too. I'm taking some to my mother and father," so we took all the meat. I was so mad. She'd only come into the family yesterday. This was my sow! Not a word to me. Killed my pig right in front of me.

Smokes

After years of going places he had to go—school, work, home, repeat—he decided today to break the mold. He wanted to go someplace else. Someplace where there was very little noise coming in from the window and from the other side of the wall. Because he was new to this neighborhood, or because it was a brown October evening quickly approaching night, or maybe because the thought just struck him at that very moment, he decided to buy a pack of smokes and go for a walk before catching the 8A bus home. He used to be a chain smoker before the wife and kids came into the picture. He used to flick the middle finger at people as they shot him nasty looks by the school door where he smoked each morning. So today, instead of going home and seeing his wife on the couch and his progeny gripping the walls and floors with their sticky fingers, he decided to take a left instead of a right and walk two blocks to the gas station to buy some smokes.

The electric door chime and stale heat greeted him as he entered and took the quick four steps to the counter. "Camels, hard pack. Regular, not lights," he instructed. The price, with tax, was $2.66. "What the fuck is this world coming to?" he thought. When he first started smoking, he could trade an even seven quarters for one pack. Now, it was two bucks and then some? What a rip-off. Thank God he didn't smoke anymore. Well, except for today.

Before he picked his smokes up off the counter, he remembered he needed a light. It pissed him off real quick that the glass-eyed old man on the other side of the counter didn't respond to him when he asked for a light. Only after his follow-up, "I said, do you have a light?" did the man point to a half-empty box of matchbooks on the edge of the counter. His dull, perfunctory gesture reminded Tou of his own life. That connection aroused a quick uneasiness in his chest, but he let it go. Poor bastard, he thought as he packed his cigarettes.

Only when he heard the smacking sound of the cigarette box hitting callused palm did the old man say with a degree of passion, "Don't do that in the store."

"'Scuse me?" Tou said.

"I said, don't do that in the store."

"Why the hell not?"

"I've been sitting here every day for the past three years, listening to that fucking sound. I'm sick of it. Now don't do that in the store."

Not wanting to start anything unpleasant, Tou left with a snarl. "What the hell was his problem? Crazy old man," he thought as the door banged shut behind him.

Back in the company of cold, sloppy leaves, he finished pounding his box. When he was done, he unwrapped the outside plastic and pulled off the shiny inner foil. Next, one slender stick was pulled out from the box and flipped around, marking it as the "lucky cigarette." With this ritual complete, he liberated one of the other "unlucky" cigarettes and brought it to his lips. When he struck the paper match against the grainy brown strip on the back of the matchbook, a phosphorous spark sounded and a brilliant light escaped.

Suddenly, he remembered an image from his past. It was a scene from his second year in college, Social Problems 1001. The class was a half-filled auditorium in the dingy Cohl Building. It was a night class made up of equal parts young and old students. Most of the young students skipped lecture on a regular basis because of a rumor that Mr. Jacobs was senile and generous with his As. What remained of the class was a handful of dazed young students, a corner of gray-haired women, a row of short-haired soccer moms, and Leah.

He had never thought of Leah as beautiful. He just saw her

as another well-intentioned white girl who talked too much. She was short and round and came into class with her coat on. Underneath her coat, she wore layers of shirts under her sweater and thick brown corduroy pants. Sometimes she wore a pair of jeans. Her stringy, ash blonde hair was tied back in a saggy ponytail. She never wore a spot of makeup. She didn't raise her hand but instead spoke freely when she thought she had something to say. Most of the time she was just thinking out loud and taking up class time. Other times, she pushed the professor into a corner and impressed the soccer moms. Tou thought she was annoying. The only reason he came to class was to get away from home on Thursdays. He didn't want to be engaged in small group discussions, grilled by class exercises, and, most of all, numbly listening to Leah.

He remembered thinking to himself in class, "What makes her think that she can question the professor in that way? What makes her think she can waste class time with her objections to the text?"

He hated the way she blurted out her questions and turned the class upside-down, taking everyone off topic just to address her concerns. In his culture that was considered selfish.

Tou was not a selfish person. When he was seventeen and found out he was going to be a father, he married Youa without question. He knew he had to get married someday; it might as well have been at seventeen. Back then he didn't question anything. He was going to drop out of school and get his GED. No sweat. He was going to respect both family names by taking a wife and working day-to-day like every other man in his house. He wasn't selfish. Not like Leah.

Now, in the chilled autumn air, prompted by the spark of a match, the memory of Leah and the reality of the present slipped side-by-side. In the match spark he saw her again, like that one evening in front of Cohl before class started. That one time when she gave him a light. She lit a match that sounded like a snap, glowed yellow in her face, and for a moment made her look less plain—almost beautiful.

He tried to shake it off, but there he was, walking in the dark, rubbing his hands to keep warm, forgetting to put his gloves on, but remembering Leah. He shivered. When he got to his bus stop, he checked his watch—less than ten minutes before the next bus would come. He pulled the short cigarette from his lips, stepped on it, replaced it with a new one, and lit it.

Inside the bus it was fluorescent bright. There was no smoking allowed, so Tou, squeezing his hand into a fist, wrung the box of seventeen cigarettes in his coat pocket. When his stop came and he got up to leave, Tou threw the mangled box and empty matchbook in the trash by the bus driver's feet. As he stepped off the bus, he thought to himself, "Thank God I don't smoke."

Hmongspeak

If you've ever been a daughter-in-law and heard your in-laws saying, "Mai [that's their daughter], clean up the house" or "Mai [same daughter], do the dishes," you know they're not really talking to Mai. They're really talking to you. It's their way of discreetly saying you need to work.

That's Hmongspeak.

Hmongspeak isn't limited to daughters-in-law or girls, however. Hmongspeak is universal. It's a way of implying something as opposed to saying things directly. The problem is that no one tells you about Hmongspeak. No one says that when parents tell you not to come home with a full belly they really mean "Don't have sex and don't get pregnant." You just have to figure it out yourself. Hmongspeak is a way of communication so culturally specific that if you can't read between the lines, you're screwed.

It's like this: I'm standing there with some relatives from my husband's side. I don't recognize any of the women, but I'm sure the experience is not entirely mutual. The Hmong have a great system of communication—if you don't consider confrontation or directness to be communication, that is. Although we have difficulty talking to our own family members, we seem to have a great network for sharing gossip and news that reaches across the country. Therefore, despite not knowing who these relatives were, I was sure they knew who I was. However, because we are not on a familiar level, they won't approach me even though we're standing right next to each other. They continue their conversations as if I'm not there.

Then one woman remarks to my husband's sister, who is standing next to me, "Eh, Mai, is your sister-in-law here?"

There: that's Hmongspeak. Of course I'm here. I'm standing right in front of her face, but she can't simply turn to me and say, "Hi, Mrs. So-and-So." No, to be truly Hmong, you've got to be discreet and beat around the bush.

Of course, Mai says, "Yes, Auntie. My sister-in-law is right here." Thus the introductions begin, and I'm no longer an ignored party.

It's hilarious, really. I don't know why we don't talk directly. Take sex for example. Hmong parents don't talk to their kids about sex. Heck, except for crude terms, I didn't learn the correct way to say sex in Hmong until I was an adult: *dag deev.* Some people prefer the even more discreet form *ua niam ua txiv:* "being husband and wife." See? Implying, assuming.

It's ironic, though: when old Hmong women are by themselves, they're so explicit it makes me blush. It makes me think, "Damn, they're not so out of the loop themselves." So, why can't they be this direct in other aspects of their lives?

At the age of twenty-five, married for eight years with two kids, I've figured out a way around Hmongspeak: ignorance, otherwise known as being direct.

At a family gathering where a sacrificial ceremony called *ua neeb* is taking place, I'm speaking to a relative about nothing important when she says, "Last week, my family *ua neeb,* too, but not many people came. We had so much work to do."

What she was really saying was, "Where the hell were you?"

Instead of saying the usual things, like "Oh, I was working" or "We were helping other relatives at their own *neeb,*" I say, "My husband and I went fishing."

The woman's brow wrinkles in wonder and disapproval at my bluntness. After all, I had put fishing before her *neeb.* As if realizing how apparent her feelings are, she rearranges her face into a mockup of pleasantness and says, "If only my husband and I had enough time as you and your husband to spend the weekend fishing. Why, there are simply too many things to do, too many people to help out."

"That is exactly why we do go fishing on the weekend. After all, there are people like you who will dutifully take care of all the dishes that need to be washed, the pigs that need to be cleaned, the pungent bathrooms that must be scoured after drunk men go through."

She looks at me with darts in her eyes. I know there is anger there, resentment that is festering, yet I also know she won't say anything—at least not to my face—or if she does say something the statement will not be anything that would satisfy her anger.

Maybe that was mean of me. I know it isn't that woman I am annoyed with. It is the whole idea of being expected to know things that were never taught to me, doing things I do not understand, and being silent, holding in the shitty things in life because we're not supposed to stand up for ourselves. That is what I was annoyed about.

Why can't people just say, "Ha ha! I'm better than you!"? It's not as if Hmong people are afraid to be mean to each other. It's okay to be mean to people behind their backs, but if everyone would just say what was on their minds, there wouldn't be kids going around saying, "My parents don't love me," or daughters-in-laws, like myself, saying, "Can't they speak to me instead of going through my husband?" Everyone would be happier.

I won't be like those people who at the age of seventy wonder out loud to their youngest son and his wife, "Aaah, I'm getting so old. Who will take care of me?" expecting them to answer back with, "Don't worry, Mom. We've got you covered." What if they say, "I don't know. Better start looking for a home, Mom"? No, I've resolved that the next time someone speaks around me instead of to me, I'll say, "Excuse me, but I have a tongue to answer for myself." Next time someone says, "I thought I saw your daughter at the park the other day," as though to imply that she's up to no good, I'll say, "That's right. I drove her there." And, if at the age of seventy my son and his wife tell me, "Start looking for a home, Mom," I'll look them straight in the eye and say, "I already found one."

The Voice

Mute. I sit alone in a world all my own, oblivious to reality, confined to thoughts and lost in dreamspaces that are untouchable to the hand. I sit in the darkness of my room, the stillness of the house. Nothing penetrates.

Whispers. There is something small knocking inside of me, jumping like it wants to crawl out.

Humming. My vocal cords are stiff because I rarely use them—but music . . . sometimes music tempts one to be lost in its rhythm.

Singing. High pitches are bad for me. I try to avoid them as best I can, for I don't want to be embarrassed if my voice cracks— Sometimes, when I am alone, I try to sing with a vibration in my voice, but high pitches? I don't even dare.

Speaking. I stutter and fumble over my words. In my mind, I speak clearly. No stuttering. No faint accents. No questioning as to what I want to say. But when speaking, I am so unsure of myself. I am no longer in solitude but interacting with the world. Sometimes the right things don't come out. I stop, take a deep breath, and start over slowly. Something inside doesn't want to quit. It is still hammering at me. Louder this time, like it wants to leap out. It is more urgent, and it won't go away. I don't think I want it to go away.

Screaming. AHHHHH! My voice has come out at last! It is like a raging storm waiting to shower itself over the world. I am not afraid of high pitches anymore. I dive into them, then my voice soars like an eagle, holding strongly onto each chord, each sound, each thought as if it were prey.

Smiling. My peaceful world could never bring a grin to my face as had the satisfaction of hearing my true voice speak out.

Kou Lor

Loneliness

1
Every time
I open my door,
I stare at the red light
on my answering machine

hoping . . .

2
I received my phone bill today
my contract with the world:
68 cents.

3
Two champagne glasses'
mouths
have been stuffed
with tissues
in their unopened box,
to quiet their whines
for wine.

4
Two cups, two plates,
two sets of silverware
have been dirtied,
but the sleuth only found
one set of fingerprints.

5
A pressed tuxedo
waits
in its closet womb
for birth.

6
Written love poems
lay under suicides
with blank spaces
where names should be.

7
A little black book
writhes from hunger pains
even though it has eaten
much chicken.

8
I sit on the edge
of my bed,
stare at a poster
of the musical *Les Misérables*—

I wait

for the phone to ring,
but I know, I know,
someone
has ripped out its tongue.

Slices with a Hmong Knife

I want to write an image poem and give you slices of who I am.
But first, I must board a plane to Laos
and I must buy a Hmong knife, forged by Hmong hands
from iron out of the belly of a sacred mountain
beside fires that consume lush green to feed Hmong mouths.

Then I must visit the village of my birth.
Perhaps the streets of earth and dust (and mud when it rains),
the single-room houses with their bamboo walls and
        bamboo-leaf roofs,
the plates of rice and meat left for spirits of ancestors,
the single spoon shared by a household during meager meals
(the spirits ate better than the living) —
perhaps all these things will help me remember
those lost nights when magical words from distant tongues
        cured all fears.

Then I must board a plan to the U.S. and
I must return to Omaha, Nebraska,
where my family first landed after our long exodus from Laos,
where our sponsors taught us how to use sinks, toilets,
        and the TV,
where I almost drowned in our sponsor's pool
and got lost from my parents in a hospital elevator.
Perhaps all these things will help me remember
my parents' half-smiles and empty faces as they were forced
        to become children again.

Then I must drive to Appleton, Wisconsin,
(as my father did only six months after arriving)
where I learned how to speak English and how to forget my
        native tongue,

where I met my first American friend and my first
    American bigot,
where I played with friends in secret places in trees
that seemed to reach their roots to Laos.
Perhaps all these things will help me remember
the grizzled face of a boy innocently torn by two cultures.

And upon arriving back in Oshkosh,
I will find that the knife is dull and I don't have
    a sharpening stone
and the traveling has left my face white like my ancestors',
so the poem must wait silently kicking in its womb
beside its growing twin, who hums quietly in Hmong.

Pacyinz Lyfoung ༀ

Walking Manifesto #2

For the First People, who never appear in any Asian American history because we too forget that before any of us—white, black, yellow—came here to argue race issues and our rights, they were here first.

I once asked a Native Hawaiian woman
What she did for a living.
She paddles canoes
Because that's what her people do.
They live on islands
Between the immensity of the sky
Above them
And the immensity of the ocean
Between them.
They salute the sun
Every morning
And spend years
Learning to read
The shades of the sun
That tell them
The difference between
Safe and unsafe crossings.

These days, I too know
That if people were to ask me,
What am I doing in life?
My response is predestined
By the people I was born into:
I walk in life
Because that's what the Hmong people
Used to do.

Having crossed the ocean,
I still walk, for justice,
Because that's what my people need.
We live in Pan Asian villages
Between the Western world
Beneath us
And the immensity of the Western culture
Around us.
I salute the spirit of my communities
And am spending my years
Learning how to read
The shades of their dreams,
Shaping the wave
That will take us all
To a true American shore
Of peace, justice, and equality.

Mai Neng Moua ⚜

Along the Way to the Mekong

Author's Note *These passages are a collection of memories from some of the first-generation Hmong students who attended St. Olaf College in Northfield, Minnesota, between 1991 and 1995.*

We thought we were going to come back. My mother hid her silver jewelry in the center of the house. She dug a deep hole underneath the stove, wrapped her jewelry in a piece of cloth, and buried it there. She promised herself that she'd someday go back for it. She never did.

⚜

My mother carried with her one duck, one chicken, one hoe, one sickle, one change of clothing each for all four of us, one bag of rice, one ax, one waterproof cloth, two blankets, two pots, four spoons, four bowls, some silver bars, seeds for two vegetables, family pictures, and medicinal seeds for constipation. All this on top of one bag of rice, plus my little brother on top of that!

⚜

My father carried me on his back the whole way.

⚜

My father was killed two years before we left Laos. My older brother was five, I was three, and my younger brother was a few months old. I had to carry a pot of rice. I don't remember what my little brother carried.

⚜

My mother carried seeds for *zaub ntsuab* and *zaub paj*. She took them out whenever we settled down for a little while and planted them wherever there was sun. She did this so we'd have greens to eat.

⚜

Along the way my aunt's leg got infected, and she couldn't walk. Some of the men said, "Give her opium to eat!" because she was slowing everyone down, but two of my uncles refused because she was not really sick. They decided they would carry her on their backs, but they couldn't for a long time. She was a big woman. No one waited for them, and they were scared. So everyone decided it was best to give her the opium. But when we got to Thailand, we heard from our cousins who were behind us that my aunt didn't die until two days later, from starvation.

⊕

We were hungry for salt and meat.

⊕

We were so hungry, my mother and I snuck back into the village that was now occupied by Vietnamese soldiers to steal food and salt.

⊕

My father told me we ran out of rice and had to resort to whatever we could find in the jungle. Sometimes, there were yams and potatoes. Other times, we took the hearts of palm trees and pounded them into a pulpy mess. We would then cook the extracted liquid and eat that in place of rice.

⊕

My father was a soldier, so he had a gun. He hunted monkeys, wild boars, and squirrels for us.

⊕

My mother didn't have a gun so she trapped crabs, lizards, birds, and fishes for us to eat. At first, all the men laughed at her, but soon she became so skilled at trapping lizards that they all came to her for advice. Sometimes, she'd look for grubs in trees for us, too. She tells me they're very good. Whatever she got, she always made sure the kids got the best portions before she herself ate, even if that meant she wouldn't be eating.

⊕

I don't remember much. Only flashes of memories, and I don't even know if they're my own. I remember it was cold, wet and cold. You know that feeling you get when your shoes are wet and you have to walk around all day with wet socks? It was like that. I remember darkness. It was always dark. There were tall trees all around. Tall skinny trees that swayed with the wind. I did not look at them because I was afraid there'd be eyes looking back at me. I remember silence. I don't remember people talking.

⁜

My father said there were lots of leeches. You couldn't just pull them off; you had to burn them off.

⁜

My mother told me that my younger brother was crying along the way. He wouldn't stop, so they gave him a little opium to keep him quiet. When they came to a rest stop and my mother took him off her back, he wasn't breathing anymore. He looked like he was just sleeping, but everyone said my mother had given him too much opium. And they took him away to be buried. The saddest thing is I don't think they even gave him a proper burial. They said they buried him, but my mother said they came back so fast. She thinks they just threw him down at the stump of some old tree.

⁜

My grandparents died along the way. They were old, and they were hungry.

⁜

Three of my uncles died. One went to find salt and never came back. Some Hmong people fighting for power killed another. And another one was ambushed. By whom? We're not sure.

⁜

My father was killed. My mother said we were always behind. By the time we got to the rest stop, everyone else would've set up tent already. They would've collected all the nearby branches and started their fires. She then had to go farther away to gather dry branches to start our fire.

⁜

I remember walking by my grandfather's side. He held my hands sometimes. Once, I fell and scraped my knees pretty bad. He pulled me up and told me not to cry.

⊹

I wanted someone to tell me things were going to be fine, but no one did.

⊹

Once, we almost left my little brother behind. I don't really remember the event. My mother told me she carried him on top of all this "stuff." He was a heavy baby, and we'd always be behind the others because he never wanted to walk. My mother had been carrying him all day, and she was tired so she took him down and told him to walk. He did but then after a little while he wanted to rest. She told him, "Okay, we will in a little bit. After that hill." We continued walking, but then he started complaining that his tummy was heavy and he was tired. He didn't want to walk anymore. My mother took him by the hand and dragged him along because it was getting dark. You couldn't see my grandpa and the others anymore, and my mother was getting scared, but my little brother refused to move. He sat down on a log, and we stopped. My mother tried to reason with him, saying, "I can't carry you anymore. You have to walk," but he wouldn't move. She told him that if he didn't walk, we'd leave without him. He didn't walk so we left. Later, the group behind us found him sitting where we'd left him. He walked with them.

⊹

I remember we had to learn how to swim. I was really scared and didn't want to, but someone threw me in the water. I had a manmade "life jacket"—a plastic bag that had been blown up and tied on the end—secured to each arm, and I was supposed to learn how to swim. I was so scared I kept trying to grab at the tree roots on the side.

⊹

We were airlifted out of Laos.

✤

My father and my sisters managed to squeeze themselves on the last available canoe.

✤

We swam our way across the Mekong. My father put me between these two pieces of bamboo, and he started swimming with me under his arm. It was dark and he couldn't see but he kept swimming. Finally, we thought we'd reached Thailand, but when my father turned back to look at the other side (which he thought was Laos), he saw lights. He knew then that we had somehow swum full circle back to Laos.

✤

My family spent three years in the jungle, hiding out. We tried four times to cross the Mekong. The first time, there were soldiers guarding the river. The second time, our Thai contacts didn't show up with the promised canoes. The third time, soldiers shot at us and we had to retreat. The fourth time, we finally made it.

✤ ✤ ✤

D.C.

I stood my ground
It's not enough that I am here
I want the imprints of their names
Some American proof that they were known
Their courage recognized
The sacrifices of their lives acknowledged

The ranger in khaki shorts and Smokey-the-Bear hat said
"You have to know someone who died there"
I stood my ground
Letting the emotions clog my throat, sting my eyes

What had I expected him to say
"Your father Tooj Cib Muas is right over here?"
My mute tongue could not scream
"But I do know someone who died there"
I know six who died there
Grandfather Soob Tseej Vws
Uncle Txooj Kuam Vws
Uncle Kim Vws
Uncle Looj Muas
Men who are supposed to be—
But are not—
Here taking care of me
Showing my little brother how to be a man

The white man had moved on
To other people—tourists gathered
Around the memorial as if
It was an exotic exhibit
Talking loudly, laughing, downing
Their Evian in the humid heat
Disturbing the memories of chaos
Just another thing you do while you're in D.C.

I stood my ground

Father Died Twenty-five Years Ago

Father died twenty-five years ago
Now mother farms a four-acre plot of land
With a tiller and a Hmong hoe
She prepares for war
Selling vegetables to white *Mekas*
In her little stall at the farmers' market
Something father would've helped her with

Father died twenty-five years ago
Now sister works two full-time jobs
To pay for the house she bought for the family
So mother would not worry
This was something father would've done

Father died twenty-five years ago
Now older brother has to be the man of the house
Struggling to finish college
He has postponed marriage and children
Mother does not trust him
She says father was a colonel at brother's age

Father died twenty-five years ago
Now younger brother has gone off to war
Leaving behind his family
As father did twenty-five years ago
Mother says he is not like father

Father died twenty-five years ago

Life in Four Short Chapters

I.
Dear Mom:
Skinniest little switches hurt most
Grit your teeth
Hold your breath
Prepare for the blow
Stinging outlines
White flesh turning
Redpurpleblack
Quick cover the wound
Protect

II.
Dear Daughter:
I retreat
Into the bedroom
And silent tears
Of a single young immigrant mother
Fall

III.
Dear Mom:
Next day, you pretend
IT didn't happen
The redpurpleblack lies
And make me breakfast

IV.
Dear Daughter:
Life for me is a kaleidoscope
Of unpaidbillsthreeyoungchildrenbrokenEnglish
Making breakfast for you
Is the only thing I can do

⚇ ⚇ ⚇

My Mother Is a Coffee Table

My mother is in the living room
And the kitchen and the bathroom
My father has gone fishing

She is on all fours
One for her three young children
Two for the unpaid bills
Three for her broken English
Four for . . . help!

With her head, she holds up the house

⚇ ⚇ ⚇

my white lover

you sit across from me
slowly smoking
your head against the wall

I pick at the sashimi with my chopsticks
wondering
if you can swallow its rawness

your blank eyes stare through me
you do not know me
I am so strange
you cannot conceive
I am alive
sitting in front of your face

I am sashimi
red and raw
you cannot swallow

there is a distant look in your eyes

♯ ♯ ♯

Endstage

Author's Note *In the summer of 1994, when I was a junior at St. Olaf College, I was diagnosed with end-stage renal disease. On August 7, 1997, I received a transplant from a Caucasian friend. This is an excerpt from a longer piece about my experience.*

I.

My mom, my two brothers, my two uncles, my cousin, and my friend are all in my room. We're waiting for the nephrologist to come talk to us. Everyone's worried. None of us know people who have kidney problems. I don't even know anything about kidneys, not really.

The nephrologist comes in, and he tells my family he wants to do a biopsy of my kidneys. Before he can finish explaining, my uncles are already shaking their heads. The doctor looks around the room and continues anyway. He shows my family the lab results.

"Her labs are ten times the norm," he tells them, but my family isn't listening. It means nothing to them. No one looks at the lab results.

"But she was okay until now," says my youngest uncle.

The older uncle says, "No, we cannot have her do that."

My mother sighs. She is worried. I can see she hasn't slept much. Her eyes are puffy, and she looks like she's lost weight since that night in the emergency room. "Me, I won't let her do that," she says.

"It's a simple procedure, really. She won't even have to go under," the nephrologist offers.

My cousin, who is a pharmacist, says, "It's not hard. I think it's a good idea to do it."

"But if we don't do it, how will we know what's wrong?" I ask.

No one answers me.

"What do you want?" the doctor asks, pointing to my uncle. "What do you want?" he says, pointing to me. "Why don't we go around the room and see what everyone wants?"

My uncles look at each other as if to say, "What's he doing?" We go around the room and, as I had suspected, only my friend, my cousin, and I agree to do the biopsy.

"If you don't want to listen to us, then why are we here?" my youngest uncle asks.

I am thinking, *Why are you here?*

II.

I have end-stage kidney disease. Both my kidneys work less than ten percent. I have to do daily peritoneal dialysis (PD) to maintain life. Now, on the right side of my stomach, a four-inch incision spews a six-inch catheter. Through the catheter, I drain 2.5 liters of dialysis solution into my body cavity. This fluid "dwells" in my body for several hours so that an exchange can take place between my blood and the dialysis solution, so that the blood is cleaned of toxins that can no longer be filtered out by my kidneys. After three to eight hours, I drain out the used dialysis solution and replace it with another 2.5 liters of solution. I do this four times a day: morning, noon, evening, and before bed.

I am mourning the loss of my body.

Shortness of breath warns of a severe asthma attack. Catch that breath. InOutInOutInOut.

In the middle of the night, my calf muscles cramp suddenly like a taut rubber band. There is nothing I can do except hold my breath, grit my teeth, and wait for the moment to pass.

Insomnia is boredom at three o'clock in the morning. In my head, a train goes round and round at top speed. Ideas, images, conversations, questions flash past my eyes like fast cars on the highway. I don't know how to turn them off.

My big tummy is a pregnant woman's. I sleep on my side,

thinking, "This is what pregnant women feel like. This is how they sleep."

Weak is warm tired arms, heavy legs, and dragging steps. I see the fumes of my life force, my physical strength, slip away from me like smoke from a chimney on a cold winter's day.

Puffy face is the girl with slits for eyes. I can't see. I force my eyes open for minutes on end but nothing, nothing changes my narrow vision. Sometimes when I wake up in the morning, my face and eyes balloon from the undrained fluid. I want to press my cheeks in until nothing but skin remains. Fluid-filled, I no longer recognize myself.

Sometimes I wonder if I am dating my boyfriend because I need to feel I am still pretty. That someone still likes me. That someone still wants me.

The scariest thing about being on dialysis is that I feel I have no control over my body. That's hard. To feel disconnected from myself. It's odd to think my own body is now a stranger to me. I am no longer intimate with my body. I cannot get attached to it because I know, I know I will lose more of it.

III.

It is the first day after the peritoneal lavage tube is placed. My mom approaches me with her herbal medicines, floating in a tall glass. It does not make any difference that I am already taking Zantac, Phoslo, Procardia, Cardura, Rolcaltrol, and Neprocaps.

She extends the glass to me.

"*Coj cov tshuaj no mus hauv hoob nab es muab ib cov ntxhua ob ceg thiab qov quav,*" she says and points to the bathroom.

"Mom, I'm sick on the inside, not . . ." How do I explain that washing myself with the herbal medicine is not going to work for kidney failure?

"*Ab, ntxhua li ntawd thiaj zoo mas. Yog muaj no tseem yuav muab ntxhua kiag yus lub cev nas,*" she continues.

I look at her and laugh out loud. I can't help it. First it was washing my hands and feet with the herbal medicine and then scraping my toenails with a knife (to relieve the pressure inside). Now she wants me to wash between my legs with the herbal medicine. How do I tell her it doesn't matter?

"It works," she insists.

"Okay, mom," I say uncertainly. I look at her again and laugh, but she only smiles. She is serious.

"*Kuv ntxhua los?*" she asks me.

"No, mom. I can do it myself," I say, laughing. Oh God, to be twenty-one and still have your mom bathe you. There is no escaping this.

My mom stands there, her hand outstretched with the herbal medicine. I take the glass and step into the bathroom. I breathe a lungful and start undressing. I sit on the cold edge of the bathtub for a long time before washing myself.

IV.

I want to move out and live with my college roommate. I know my mother does not want me to. She says, "*Ua cas es yuav xav mus ua tej yam qias neeg thag npauv!*"

"What 'dirty' things would I do, *niam?*" I ask her.

She thinks I'm going to invite over all the men I know and have wild parties. She's worried that other Hmong people will say bad things about me, an unmarried Hmong woman living "by herself."

"*Twb mob npaum es tseem yuav mus dab tsi nas?*" she asks. She doesn't understand why I, a sick person, would want to move out on my own.

"*Nyob no es kuv mam take care koj nas,*" she tells me. She's concerned that I won't be able to take care of myself. She's afraid that I won't have enough money to pay rent, buy food, or pay bills.

I know my older brother does not want me to move out. When I ask him about it, he says, "Why do that to mom? After all she's been through, isn't it time we took care of her? Doesn't she deserve more?"

I know my uncles and relatives do not want me to move out. At a family gathering, my aunt, who had heard the news from my mother, makes the announcement that I want to move out. There is an immediate rush of whispers. One of my uncles asks why I want to live by myself.

"There is no room for me," I tell them. "I want to go to grad school, and I need a quiet place to study. I don't want to study at the kitchen table with all the dishes!"

My explanations are no good. They've already made up their minds. I am bombarded with suspicion.

"Don't you love your family?"

"Don't you want to take care of them?"

"Didn't you hear about that Vang girl that was living by herself? Don't you know what people say about her?"

"You can't do that. We won't let you."

"Stay home."

It's true. The two-bedroom apartment is too small for my mom, my two grown brothers, and me. It's true that I want to go to graduate school. What I cannot tell them is that I need to move out on my own because I want to learn how to take care of myself. I want to know how to balance school, work, and dialysis. I don't want to be a burden to my family. I don't want them to worry about who's going to take care of me, the sick one. I need to know that I can pay my own bills. I don't have the Hmong words for these thoughts, and so I do not say anything. Besides, they've already made up their minds. No explanation will be good enough for them anyway. I have no defenses. There is nothing I can do but cry.

V.

I am on the waiting list for a cadaver kidney. I am told the average wait is two years but many Asians, many Hmong people, do not donate. I have to wait at least another year and a half. I may have to wait longer.

It seems kind of strange that my own family will not donate a kidney when my friends have offered me their kidneys. I am not sure how to respond to or feel about these offers. At first, I am skeptical. I think, "Everyone feels sorry for me. They're just trying to be nice." But when I find out that they are serious, I want to cry. I want to ask them, "How can you give me one of your kidneys? You're not my family." I want my family to give me a kidney.

Sometimes, I feel like my family is punishing me for not listening to them—for not choosing herbal medicine over dialysis—by making me wait the two years for a cadaver kidney. I mean, I know why they don't want to give me a kidney. They're scared. My mom won't even let my brothers get tested because she said it's better to just have one person sick than to have two. I guess she's right, but you only need one kidney to live; you're not going to get sick or die if you donate one. I know they're afraid, but it doesn't change the fact that I need a new kidney. I need a new kidney.

VI.

I am here again. And I am still scared. Scared of the surgery to take out the PD catheter. Will it hurt? Will it leave a scar? Scared I won't wake up after surgery. Scared of the IVs. Scared because no one is here with me. I am alone.

I am sad, and I don't even know why. It's too complicated. Like that passage in Richard Wright's *Black Boy* when his mother tells him they're going to take a trip down the river. He's expecting a great boat and a great ride, but when they finally get down to the river and the boat turns out to be an ugly old boat, he is so disappointed and angry that he starts crying. His mom asks him what's wrong, and it's so complicated he can't even explain it. It goes so far back that he doesn't even know where to start. It's that kind of complicated today.

My mom is worried and angry. I am angry, too. Last night, I called to tell her I was coming in for surgery—to take out the old PD catheter because it was infected and making me sick. I have to put a new permanent catheter in my shoulder so I can do hemodialysis instead of peritoneal dialysis.

My mom said, "It's up to you. Whatever you want to do . . ." What did I expect her to say? "Don't do it. I know a better way . . ."? Shouldn't I have been glad she gave me permission to do what I wanted? All my life, it seems, I've been fighting for this exact thing. But then I think, "Please care. Tell me what to do. Don't say, 'It's up to you.'" Sometimes when she says this, I feel like she's punishing me. An irritated, "Well, you chose this path, so why are you asking me what to do?" An angry, "Well, you didn't listen to me. See what happens?!"

My mother thinks I work too much, too hard. She's right. I do work two part-time jobs. Working is normal. Going to meetings with people is normal. Teaching creative writing is normal. Dancing at Gay 90's is normal. Normal is dating. Normal is going to school. And so in the fall of 1994 I go back to St. Olaf to finish my last year, despite kidney failure and my mother's protests. I take a full load of classes; I work ten hours a week; I am president of the Asian Student Association; I perform with a social justice theatre group; I work with an anti-racism group; I come home on weekends for *Paj Ntaub Voice*, the literary arts magazine I started.

My mother says, "You're working like a healthy normal person, someone who's not sick. Stop working. Go on SSI. Stay home. Go to the library. Read. Do a little interpreting for the doctors."

She thinks that because I have end-stage renal disease, I am disabled. She sees me as a loss to her, to the family, to the Hmong community, to society in general. I mean, I can still work but I won't be able to do it as fast, as well, as hard, or as much.

She says, "A disabled person like you . . . who would want to marry you? A good daughter-in-law gets up early and cooks for the family. You won't be able to do that . . ."

She's right. I won't.

VII.

Sometimes when I see my older relatives, they remark, "Oh, you're much better!" They think I am better because I am up, not lying down in a hospital bed.

I want to shake them and scream, "I'm still sick!" I want to show them the six-inch catheter that hangs out of the right side of my stomach that I have to tape in place after every peritoneal dialysis exchange. Or perhaps they'd like to see the second one, the one hanging from my right shoulder that's used for hemodialysis?

My older relatives think I am much better because I am walking.

I want to give them a piece of my dialysis-preoccupied mind that is consumed with the effects of dialysis on my body. There is no rest from these thoughts when my whole body is affected by dialysis. Every morning, I see it in my puffy face and eyes. I feel it in my tummy of 2.5 liters of fluids and my water-filled cheeks, ankles, and legs.

My older relatives think I am much better because I am working.

I want them to come to my twice-a-month doctor's appointments and visit all the medical people I have to see. I want them to take meds every morning, before every meal, and every evening. I want to give them the EPO shots I have to take to stimulate my bones to make more red blood cells. The shots that I cannot give myself because they sting and bring tears to my eyes. The ones that make me forget to go to the nurse's office every Friday when she's supposed to give me the shot in my right arm while distracting me with questions about classes.

My older relatives think I am much better because I am driving.

I want them to feel the despair in my soul when I've done everything the doctors have told me to and followed every direction to a T, and I still get sick, and they don't know why, and they don't know how I can prevent it from happening next time. I want them to have peritonitis, when I have diarrhea, and I throw up, and I have chills, and my tummy is so raw and sensitive it bounces back when I gently touch it.

My older relatives think I am much better because I look all right. There is no open wound. Nothing is bleeding.

I want to show them the clothes that no longer fit me, the closet full of dialysis boxes and supplies, the medical waste I hide in the garbage can, praying that the garbage man never looks too closely. I want them to experience the sleepless nights when I cannot turn off the ideas, images, conversations, and questions. Or the nights when I have nightmares after taking the doctor's pills which are supposed to help me sleep. They never did.

Epilogue

As I reflect back on my experiences with end-stage renal disease, I feel so old. It's hard to believe that I went through all of that "stuff." Sometimes, the whole thing is surreal to me. I feel as if it's another person's story and not my own.

It's been quite a lonely journey. Many times I wanted to share my suffering and my fear with my family and relatives, but I did not want them to worry. I had moved out with my college roommate, and I did not want them to force me to move back home. It was important for me to live on my own. I wanted time to understand what I was going through, to try to make sense of it all. I know I have hurt and isolated many people, including my family, because of my decisions, but they were the only ones I could live with, literally.

Because my donor, Eric, is Caucasian, his decision to donate surprised the Hmong community. They did not understand why he would do it. He was not Hmong; he was not family; he was not my boyfriend or my husband. Our decision to go ahead with the transplant touched the lives of many Hmong people, especially those in my church, and altered many stereotypes about white people as well.

Although I am doing very well now because of my transplant, I know many of my relatives still question my decision. Even though none of them ever talk to me about it, I know they worry about what I will do when this one fails. I worry about it, too, but I have lived through so much, I'm sure I'll live through that, too.

Vayong Moua ✐

The Hmong Wall

In the sixteenth century, in order to keep the Hmong from venturing outside
Kweichow, the Ming dynasty constructed the Hmong Wall, a smaller version
of the Great Wall of China that was one hundred miles long, ten feet tall, and
manned by armed guards.

Anne Fadiman, The Spirit Catches You and You Fall Down

Perhaps I will not destroy the Hmong Wall, but I already have
plans to climb it and break off a piece to bring back to my parents. I'll say to them proudly, "This is how much you were
feared. A powerful emperor and dynasty created this for you
and me. Not for Attila the Hun, Alexander the Great, or Genghis
Khan, but for you and me. I've brought this rock back to show
you what you've already overcome and that, though history has
not been kind to us, we have persevered against war, tragedy,
and displacement."

In fact, I don't even know where Kweichow is exactly, but
I suspect it's in southwestern China somewhere. No matter, it
can't hide behind centuries of amnesia or even archaeological
sensitivity. Call it vandalism or disrespect for national historical
artifacts, but believe me, the Hmong Wall will be conquered.
It'll be climbed, even if I have to evade guards and tourists or
set out at midnight. Do I sound resentful, angry, or overzealous?
On the contrary, my initial reaction upon learning about the
Hmong Wall was *pride*. You see, I understood we had had a series
of civil wars with the Hans, but I never thought they viewed
us as an imperial threat. We were not little annoying ants to
fend off; we commanded respect, labor, anxiety, and significant
resources as a serious adversary. I'm not proud to be an enemy,
but I am proud to be taken seriously as human beings and a cultural force. Ironically, though, we never wanted China, only
autonomy.

When I stood on the Great Wall of China as a student, I was
amazed at the labor and energy invested in its construction. But

what really fascinated me was the psychological wall ingrained in the Chinese at that time, and, in fact, in all societies consumed with war, territory, and power. I was struck with wonder and humility before such a gigantic human construct, but I felt no personal liberation. But the Hmong Wall poses itself as a personal attack on my legacy, my ancestors, and my identity. This is not academic rhetoric or global exploration, but rather an act of defiance in the name of my people. And so, with the risk of being blinded with superficial nostalgia and redemptive adventure, the climb is on!

◌ ◌ ◌

The Shadow that Loved

Author's Note *This short piece was primarily inspired by Shel Silverstein's book* The Giving Tree. *It also makes some allusions to the contrasts between Eastern and Western philosophies on nature. Although having considerable admiration for* The Giving Tree, *I arrived at the end with a sense of shame at being human and felt that the human character needed some kind of redemption and moral resurrection. This story is my way of returning a gift to a tree that loved irrationally and yet with tremendous creativity and life force.*

One day, a traveler from the east stopped to rest in a green forest overflowing with life. As he entered the forest, he noticed a naked tree, bare and weak. All around this tree were many luscious and fruitful trees, but none of them were close enough to offer shade. It looked as if a boundary was purposefully set for death. A circle of sparse brown grass, dried soil, and dead branches surrounded the tree. No buds were apparent on the tree, but it still was not dead. It stood there like a crucified tree, looking like an outcast freak shamed by the forest.

The silent man could not accustom himself to the sight—vulnerable, lonely, and suffering, he thought. Perhaps he saw himself in that tree. He wept as he approached the tree and brought with him a cool piece of cloth to wrap around the trunk. The tree badly needed protection from the brutal sun, unlike the trees with leaves, which celebrated each day because their trunks could enjoy the shade. When the cloth dried up, the man went to a nearby pond to replenish the cloth for the tree. Years went by, and he did this every day, nurturing the tree until sundown. He even tried planting friends around the tree, but the soil was so impoverished that none could grow. One year there was a harsh drought and the sun became very selfish. It wanted to shine all the time and forgot its connection to everything. Even the full trees began to fade into brown. All life in the forest was dealt a heavy blow. But for the naked tree especially, it seemed unbearable. Death would be inevitable now.

The man from the east trembled in anxiety and helplessness. He embraced the tree, spreading his short and thin body to provide a shadow to cover as much of it as possible; every inch of bark he could shield from that ruthless sun was precious. He'd close his eyes and only when he could feel evening coming would he pull down his armor. He'd depart in the evening with great fear, wondering if the tree would live until the next day. Although he could not hear the tree, he knew it was crying. The sun became hotter and stronger, so hot that the earth around the tree had dried up and small cracks gave way. The eastern man wondered why this tree never budded leaves or died. It seemed to just stay in a coma-like state, like a lame animal suffering but unwilling to die.

The man from the east got older and weaker, but his determination to protect the tree grew stronger. He wouldn't go home and stayed with the tree day and night. He left his family and friends for his beloved tree. He clung so tightly to the tree that his skin was covered with bark crumbles and, if you looked closely enough, you could see the impression of the tree on him. The man did not squint as the sun tried to stare him down. He looked like a mother clinging to a dead child. Soon, he became like the tree: bare, abandoned, yet willing life to return. And so, one day the eastern man collapsed from exhaustion. His body looked like a root of the tree, brown and convoluted. He lay at the base of the tree with his cheek still pressed against the trunk. His hands folded together on the other side of the tree, looking like they were about to slip, but they would not. All trees in the forest were lifeless and colorless now. It seemed as if even a gentle breeze could blow the trees over.

So now, it became a naked forest with a lonely tree and man at the center. Then, a man passing by from the west took rest in the forest. He fell asleep and forgot a piece of glass in the open. That made the sun smile and raise his brow. Here was his chance to strike the final blow, the sun thought. The sun pushed away all the clouds in preparation for the kill. With the help of that glass, a spark was born and started dancing. It took only one touch of the flame to begin the massacre. Waves of orange and yellow crashed into the forest. A quick friendship was made between the wind and flames, creating a choir singing with high-pitched screams and eerie cracks. It was a massacre of the already wounded, of the already dying.

The flames swallowed the western man with no real satisfaction. He was merely in the way. His bottle, picnic basket, and umbrella were of no comfort to him anymore. They lay black and crisp near him, loyal companions to the grave.

When the eastern man awoke from his exhaustion, he noticed that he was covered entirely in gray. Was it winter, he thought, mistaking ashes for snow. Astonished, he gently brushed off the ashes and gazed at the destruction. He couldn't tell what time it was. The sun was not up, nor was it down. All of the forest was charred and brittle. When he shook off his daze, the silent man searched his beloved tree for any trace of wounds and pain. Remarkably, because no other trees or plants extended close enough to the naked tree, the blaze had had no path to travel.

The naked tree stood unharmed from the devastation, only sprinkled with ashes. The eastern man rejoiced in relief, for his beloved tree had survived. The tree stood apart from the forest and so could not be determined by the forest. And because of its loneliness and solitude, it was able to cultivate the will to live and the spirit of independence.

As time went by, the sun was tempered by the other elements and returned to his place. Years went by, and the man became older. He no longer had clothes and hair. His skin became wrinkled and rough. For much of its life, the tree had no leaves and relied on the man for shade and cultivation. But it could no longer bear the sight of this waning shadow that had loved it for so long. Its gratitude was yearning to be released. The tree soaked up as much sun and water as possible and conjured all of its will to flourish and grow. Suddenly, the old man felt a cool sensation blanketing his leg. He looked carefully and saw a small shadow of a leaf on his leg, and then another, and another! Soon, his entire body was covered with shade. Above him was a vibrant and thick canopy. He saw leaves and branches twisting upward. Leaves were bursting all around him in a celebration. Looking up into the canopy, he could see only small glittering openings of the sky. It was a web of green, blue, and brown, spotted with sparkles of light. The old man gave a sighing smile. He looked up for only a moment. Although he admired the mosaic of colors above him, he closed his eyes and cherished the consoling shade. For so long, he was a shadow; finally, the tree could be a shadow.

The silent man released his spirit into the tree. Later, his body would follow and become part of the tree. Now, he could always be a shadow for those who were weary and needed rest.

The naked tree was no more. It still stood alone, but it had the life force of an entire forest. Many fires came and went, but the lonely tree always remained. Many travelers from the east and west passed by and rested in its shade. Many spirits were comforted and sheltered from storms and the sun, all because there was a shadow that loved.

Noukou Thao ᓍ

The Garden

She did not visit her parents often. They lived in the country,
up in Appleton, Wisconsin, and she lived in the city, down in
Chicago. After college, she chose to accept a position at an up-
and-coming financial corporation in Chicago, as far away from
the obligations and demands of home as possible. Her parents
lived with her older brother and his family. She felt, being a
middle child among five children, that she could afford the lux-
ury of keeping an apartment in the city, away from family. Her
brother was expected to care for her parents into their old age,
until her younger brother and his wife had their family; then
they could care for her parents.

Since she was promoted to Regional Finance Manager of
New Acquisitions, she—laptop in front of her, cell phone tucked
delicately into her soft leather Coach bag, and nude Chanel lipstick on her lips—was on top of the world.

She had a boyfriend at one time, but that was long ago. She
did not need a man. She did not need her sister to nag at her for
choosing a career over family, or her brother to remind her to
check her oil. In the city, she was her own woman.

Although busy, at long intervals—sad, thoughtful, senti-
mental moments—she considered her parents and their toil over
their Hmong vegetables during the laborious summer months.

And so one weekend, on a whim, in August, she got into
her midnight blue Lexus IS300 and started north to Wisconsin.

There, she greeted her little nephews and nieces with happiness and joy. She had been away long, and they had grown.
Gina was now in fourth grade, Amy was going into sixth grade,
and Philip was in first grade. The older two, Jenny and Mason,
were in eighth and ninth grades. These were her older brother
Lou's children. He and his wife worked at a factory in Appleton.

"How come you never come home anymore?" her younger
brother asked her at dinner that night, after her four-hour drive

83

north from Chicago to Appleton. He had just stepped into the house from tossing the basketball outside with Mason.

"I'm trying to get ahead," she told him, "you know that."

"Didn't you say that two years ago?"

"I'm still rising," she said to him. He didn't understand her grueling hours, her minute-to-minute meeting schedules, her fifteen-minute on-the-run lunches, her five-minute showers in the morning, her race to beat traffic in the early Chicago sun. He didn't understand a thing about her life. And she didn't understand his: married at eighteen to a wife that he didn't seem to care much about. But he was excited about the baby they were having.

He didn't understand that since she started with the corporation she had been fighting tooth and nail against Northwestern graduates. She had graduated from the University of Wisconsin with a business degree and was finishing her M.B.A. at DePaul's very competitive finance program. Her company was financing her M.B.A., so she had to keep up with her studies, plus be quick at her job and on the ball enough to demonstrate mobility within the corporation. She had to stay ahead, had to stay wide awake in the game. She didn't want to nap like some lower and middle managers and not speed her way vertically, shooting up in this age of mega-mergers and digital millionaires. In this day and age, if you blink, you're out of the loop.

Chicago Business Monthly said if you aren't a millionaire by the time you're thirty, you might never be one. She was twenty-seven and counting. Within the year she would gain a little stock in the corporation and be the brain behind all the new e-commerce accounts: a locked asset among her young colleagues, indispensable.

Although she wasn't the first female in her family to graduate from college, she was going to be the first to become a six-figure executive, and within the first three years of her career! (This was notable, considering that she lived in the Midwest and that she was a minority with barriers to shatter through before taking each step, even in this, the digital age!) Not bad for a member of a family that arrived in this country with nothing in their pockets but the three bars of silver that her father and mother had lovingly wrapped in an old blue wool handkerchief. Fresh from the Vietnam War, the silver bars shone like the bettas that swam in the streams of Thailand.

They had nothing when they first arrived in Milwaukee. They lived on public assistance. Her father used to get lost going downtown when he accompanied her mother to renew their family's food stamp application. They needed a Hmong volunteer from Lutheran Social Services to go with them to interpret when Mee, her older sister, was in school. Mee was the smart one of her two older siblings. She was always expected to be the voice. Although her eldest brother, Lou, was strong, he was silent, very silent, like her father. He seemed to have fallen into fatherhood without half as much of a whistle, barely graduating from high school and stopping forty-five credits short of a technical school certificate, so he was supporting a family of seven plus some on nine dollars an hour, non-unionized.

Her father—the farmer, the silent soldier who never spoke a word about the war, the war that killed his older brother, his younger brother, his cousins, and the part of his heart that he left in the old country—lived on social security now.

Her mother was more talkative. She was White Hmong and could talk faster than her husband, although after all these years her voice had changed its contours to blend into the tones of the Green dialect of her husband's Her clan.

"You never come home, you never come home," her mother would singsong to her in a White-turned-Green-accented Hmong voice.

"Come home," her father would say to her gently, while he sharpened the knife blade out in their back yard. He was going to the garden to chop some branches to support the tomato vines and prevent them from leaning so much to the side toward the dusty ground as their fruit ripened.

"Come to the garden with us, and I will pick some beans, tomatoes, and cucumbers for you. You can boil the corn ears later," her mother beckoned her.

Although ordinarily she did not accompany her parents to the garden, during this trip, in the heat of the escalating summer sky, she decided to go.

There, out in the open field, she saw the fruit of her parents' labor. Sleeping all around the far corner of the field were cucumber vines spreading their arms; near the corn stalks that were starting to dry out a little the tomatoes were ripening. The beans were now their full lengths, growing in bundles along the straight lines of her parents' one-acre lot of earth.

"Wow," she thought, "where did my parents learn how to farm like this?"

Where had she been all their lives? How had she never really seen their garden before?

At ten o'clock, she went to the garden with her parents. They did not farm in straight lines; they farmed in wiggly lines. They did not plant cabbage heads. The other Hmong people, who also had land near her parents' garden acre, did not plant wild flowers either.

Now, almost seventeen years later, her parents' garden acre looked different. She was amazed, deeply and quietly amazed.

"Mom, I only want a couple," she said, referring to the corn.

"No, take more," her mother insisted, stuffing ear after ear into a plastic Target bag for her. "Here, wear this."

Still, she, alone in Chicago in her high-rise, one-bedroom apartment overlooking Lincoln Park, with no one around but American friends and every now and then Vietnamese and Korean girlfriends coming over for weekend Italianfest dinners and white wine, could not eat that much food.

Her mother threw her a gardening glove to pick cucumbers with. She wanted a couple of the smaller ones for her salads at home when she made her infamous spaghetti sauce. She wanted to pick cilantro for garnish and for seasoning. She had been away for far too long. She could be saving all those trips to the corner grocery store, if only she would start her herb pots.

From the corner of her eyes she noticed her father bending down to examine a bean plant to make sure that he had plucked all of the beans from that specific little bush. He and her mother were quietly at work. After collecting a couple more nicely shaped prickly cucumbers, she stood up in the middle of the field.

She felt a quiet southern wind blow near her ear, whispering, "The garden, the garden. . . ." In the silence of its song, she heard, "Come home to the garden."

She ended up carrying more than thirty ears of corn and a pail of green beans plus two Target bags of cucumbers and forty-five tomatoes back to Chicago.

Driving home on the highway heading south that Sunday afternoon, listening to an old song from the eighties—Laura Branigan singing "Solitaire"—she started to cry.

"I will always go home now," she thought, "every year I will return to my parents' garden and the earth, to pick my parents' vegetables."

The True Tale of Yer

A small horde of portly blackbirds is huddled on the trash bin behind my home on Edmund Avenue. Their lustrous plumage is as slick as crude oil. They are a brutish pack of mourners in their Sunday best, tittering away freely as they pick about with a ghoulish gourmet's discretion.

Their raucous conversation comes to an abrupt halt as I approach, and we meet each other's eyes with deep mutual suspicion and contempt.

As a young child in Anchorage, Alaska, I learned from the locals that the Inuit have a name for such birds, which are larger than your ordinary crow, raven, or rook. The whites couldn't twist their tongues to pronounce the word, so they transliterated it to the name "Soul Chickens."

Before the white men arrived, the Soul Chickens were notorious for descending on scenes of human death and misery in the frozen lands to the north. The Inuit believed these dark-feathered fiends came to eat your soul through your eyes, pecking them out with their cold, sharp beaks.

The creatures would be less defamed if they didn't laugh so much as they dine. In times of great hunger, they don't even have the courtesy to wait for you to be dying if they discover you alone on a dark night, beyond the sight of civilized society.

When the white men arrived to "settle" Alaska, the Soul Chickens spread their massive wings to descend on the huge piles of garbage these men created, gorging themselves with delight. As a child, I was deeply troubled to think what part of the human soul these creatures had found worth feeding on in our trash.

My mother warned me to give them a wide berth back then. It was unwise to cross creatures with such an unsavory reputation. I remember the unsettling encounter I had one day as I walked home through a snowstorm after school, trying to find my mother, who was supposed to be waiting on the corner for me.

The trees were bare bleached skeletons, arrayed like a silent army on the sides of the road, and hideous laughter could be heard all around the neighborhood. The reassuring rattle and roll of traffic, of rusting engines and giant snow tires, lumbered by all too infrequently. When I finally saw my mother, I was relieved. But a Soul Chicken had seen me, too, and rose up from the neighbor's garbage, flapping its great wings toward me. It flew over my head and began circling above, its dark eyes evaluating me like a surgeon about to make his first incision.

I quickly ran to my mother, who hurried me inside. My long trek through the storm was not without cost, however: I had caught a horrible case of pneumonia, which kept me hospitalized for several months. From my bed, I watched Soul Chickens chuckle, watching me with hungry eyes through the windows into my ward.

When my family moved to the Midwest a few years later, I thought I had put Soul Chickens behind me. But today I am an adult in the dingy streets of Frogtown, and there they are, clustering nearby with an avian wink. Ravenous as ever.

Perhaps these are only distant cousins making themselves at home on my trash, but it makes little difference to me. I loathe the obscene things and spit toward them with all of the venom I can muster. One flies off with an audacious caw, circling overhead. The others erupt into laughter and soon return to the more important matter of eating my refuse.

I glance down at the melting snow around my driveway. It strikes me that peculiar shapes have formed in the puddles on the blacktop beneath the afternoon sun. Perhaps it is only my imagination, but it seems all too easy to discern scenes ripped from a Boschian vision of hell—agonized skulls, leering specters, and other grisly hints of a stygian underworld.

I hurry to ascend the stairs to my apartment on the second

floor before the last light of day dissipates. The hallway light is flickering and threatens to plunge the entire passage into utter darkness.

From behind closed doors I hear the chatter of my neighbors in broken English and Khmer on one side and raspy, exasperated Hmong on the other. The aroma of Cambodian cooking is engaged in a bloody fistfight with the scent of Hmong cuisine in the stairwell, rising higher, ever higher.

My neighbors have complained to me at different times about the others' stench. I simply shrugged and promised each of them I would look into it.

When I first moved to my apartment six months ago, I discovered that the previous tenants had hung an ear of Indian corn and a small sachet of peculiar herbs and powder on the back door, which had been badly marred in the past by deep scratches and dents. My neighbors informed me that a Hmong shaman had told my predecessors to do this to ward off evil spirits.

Given the circumstances under which they had so abruptly left, according to the local gossip, I was never too certain of the charms' effectiveness. At least the rumors of a haunted apartment made the landlord amenable to a reasonable rate for the monthly rent.

At some point today, the corncob had fallen. Dozens of dried kernels had broken off, creating a parti-colored mess of crimson and black on the floor.

I kneel down to pick up the sad charm, idly replacing it on its hook. I turn the brass key to the door, which, as usual, sticks until you give it a good hard twist. Finally, the door gives way to my apartment, a cavernous steal at five hundred dollars a month in this part of town. When my family helped me move in here, they thought it was too spacious for just one person, but I paid little heed to their objections. The location was too perfect to be believed, just blocks away from the Metro Transit's #16 bus line to my work.

I enter the kitchen to cobble together something for dinner. Not surprisingly, the refrigerator is bare, save for a few lonely cans of half-finished soda and a plastic tub of *laab*, a spicy beef salad similar to steak tartar, that I had purchased from one of the many restaurants on University Avenue. Nestled among some wilting lettuce leaves, a squeezed wedge of lime, and a sprig of mint, the *laab* is waiting impatiently for me finish it off before it goes bad.

I oblige, only to find that it is already rotten. Retching, I quickly dispose of the rest of the *laab* in the trash can. I hurry into the bathroom to brush my teeth. Spitting out the last of the foul meat, now mingling in my mouth with minty-fresh toothpaste, I hear a strange noise. I turn around and am horrified at the hideous thing before me.

"Only dogs have white teeth," a hulking creature of feline visage snarls in contempt. Its dark, blotchy fur reeks of bloody filth and waste, and it's taking my best effort to keep from vomiting at the sight of this abomination in my hallway. It stands hunched over at nearly six feet tall, with eyes like glittering opals. Its jagged, stained teeth barely fit into its gruesome maw. Its breath comes in a strange, ragged rhythm, and it grooms itself with a long, prehensile tongue. "My master insists you give him an audience, Storyteller," it hisses, reaching for me. I try to scream, but no sound comes out as I scramble away from its outstretched claw. My efforts to evade it are futile.

It picks me up effortlessly, and I am hustled roughly into my living room, pressed onto my knees. I feel cold, chilled to the bone by what is happening, and I want to hurl myself out of the window. But I am held firmly in the monstrosity's iron grip.

"Storyteller," I hear a deep voice rumble. I watch as the ebony shadows before me solidify into slithering dark slugs wriggling their way onto my couch. The air has grown foul with the mixed stench of unseen viscera and incense. The room is growing colder, and I can see my own breath, even though it is spring. I want to wake myself out of this awful dream!

"You are not dreaming. We have come. And you will tell the world what you have seen, Storyteller. If you please us, you will live to see the morning. Perhaps."

"This can't be happening!" I say aloud, wondering if I have gone insane.

"It can, and it is," comes the rumbling reply.

The shadows have coalesced into the shape of a massive creature, an unholy hybrid of man and tiger, its muscles rippling with ferocious power and supernatural malevolence. Around me, I can feel the presence of hundreds of cruel eyes upon me, watching me, ready to tear me into a thousand scarlet shreds at a single command. My eyes turn toward the wall and the picture of my family, who gaze at me impotently, powerless to help.

"Who—who are you?" I stammer, trying not to sound like a fool.

"Who do you think I am, Storyteller?" the tiger creature rumbles in reply.

"I—I don't know . . ." I say, flinching as I see the rage flood into his eyes, pouring into those cold pupils like a pitcher of boiling blood. It is clearly the wrong answer.

"I have walked with you and your ancestors for four thousand years! Before your kind could even keep time!" he roars. "I am the spirit you trembled in terror of for generations upon generations! It is to me that you fed the worst of your pitiful kind. I am he whose name you whispered fearfully to your children at night to make them behave! And now, you do not recognize me? What insolence! What arrogance, this creature, man!"

The room fills with ominous growling and inhuman shouting from every corner. My guard's gruff gnarled hands grow colder, tightening. I feel its teeth draw closer, and it is salivating in anticipation. It's impossible. I can't be here. Nothing my family had ever spoken of had prepared me for this.

"This can't be real! You're not real. You're just a myth! That's all! You're just a bit of badly digested beef!" I cry out, shaking my head in denial.

A terrifying roar silences me, as the seething demonic figure raises a massive hand in outrage, ready to strike me for my affront.

"I am the Tiger King, Storyteller! Do you dare not recognize me now? In your heart, you know this to be true. And I have come a million miles to tell you what I tell you tonight. To align the records properly and bring your kind a final gift from my dying court. You will mark these words exactly, or we shall tear you apart on the day of your greatest happiness."

"Forgive me!" I say, trembling before the beast's forbidding presence, trying to assuage its anger. "I don't mean to offend you. Please, let me live. Please, tell me what you want!"

"Well," the Tiger King says, slowly calming down. My horrible guard's hands relax ever so slightly. "Were we not bound by such short time, I would not be contented so easily, Storyteller; know this to be true. But we are dying, and this has brought me to you."

"Surely the Tiger King cannot die," I say.

"My servants in this world grow few and thin. My people hold not even half the fear you gave us when we all were young. I blame this on many things, especially the gun and grenade. But we cannot return the Djinn of Arabia to their bottles, and we great tigers must one day fade from this world into myths for your puling kin," says the Tiger King somberly.

"But before we leave this kingdom of flesh and mud, we shall tell you the truth of one of your oldest tales. We owe you this much, for a thousand years of your fearful hearts."

Rough laughter fills the room.

"But why me, great Tiger King? Surely there are others . . ."

"Do not dare question me, Storyteller!" the Tiger King barks. "Do you think you can tell a single story and not have it come back to my palace? Do you think there is a word you mortals can whisper that I do not know about? We have watched you from the first day you were born to this, and we know your ears, eyes, and tongue are the perfect vessel by which to deliver our tale. Fail me in this, Storyteller, and your soul will know agony as the hells of man have never seen."

With that admonition, the Tiger King begins to tell his awful tale, and I can do nothing but remember and take his words within my own heart.

"In the plains of ancient Qin that you now call China, before the Three Kingdoms and before the fabled Yellow Emperor was even a thought, your people had settled down to build a civilization greater than any had seen. What ambition that was! I and my brethren watched from the high hills and forests, waiting to see what would come of it all, anxious to begin our greatest feasts.

"The great Zaj, too, watched curiously from the distance as you cut and carved your homes from wood and earth, making your fires, drawing your water from their streams. It was all quite impressive, though little did you know what jealousy it would spark in the hearts of your neighbors, centuries later.

"Among the great families of the Hmong, there was one man whose face I'll always remember. But your people only remember his daughter, Yer. Such a strange thing, the human memory. She was a chubby little morsel . . . um, mortal.

"Her father was an esteemed hunter, greatly admired by my people for his savage ferocity in battle, his cunning, his patience, his stealth. Would that the heavens had made him a tiger! You all might have been living beneath our feet instead.

"To us, he was a peculiar human, without fear and possessed of a taste for raw blood unlike any we'd seen before. Few of us would have thought of challenging him, even alone in the woods. But one afternoon, drunk on blood wine, my brother, on his way home, came upon the hunter and called out a greeting to him. But the hunter saw this kind gesture instead as an attack, a challenge to the death.

"Your tales say he fell to my brother, and that my brother disguised himself in his clothes, heading to the man's house. But I tell you now, this was not so! It was my brother who died that awful day, his bones left for the birds to peck at without even a word of remorse, slit open from belly to eye by that accursed hunter's knife.

"But something had changed in the hunter. No, not changed. Simply awoken. Certainly, all of the polite formalities of human conversation were observed as he sat down to eat with his family. Certainly, nothing was too amiss. He liked his meals with extra blood in them, but his wife had grown used to this over the years. He played roughly with his children, but that time was a terrible period in human history, and everyone, even children, had to be raised to be tough enough to endure the harsh beatings that reality would provide in due time.

"I had heard rumors that the hunter had a mistress, but I've never seen this proven true. Rumors are like little children for you humans. You make them at every opportunity, it seems. But this has little bearing on the story that you know.

"That night, our worlds changed forever, as the hunter became filled with an insatiable hunger from the deepest pit of his maniacal stomach. He took his knife, still caked with my brother's blood, and began carving his family apart, eating their hearts, their eyes, their tongues, even their livers, gnawing on their bones with a sickening crunch. We could smell the carnage even within the deepest chambers of my palace of shadows.

"He threw their fat into a black iron pot above the fire, and we could hear it sizzling with a blasphemous hiss. The hunter's daughter, Yer, awoke from all of the noise to see him gnawing on her mother's severed arm. She cowered in her room, wetting herself. And soon, her father turned his attentions to her, unaware of how much she knew.

"As he approached her, he called, 'Yer! Yer! Your father wants to see you . . .' But she would not be fooled. She took a nearby bowl of hot peppers and flung them into his eyes. He screamed in agony, and she ran past him, bolting out of the door, looking for help.

"When she finally found help, they rushed to her house and secretly peered inside through a hole in the wall. They were horrified at the scene, for her father was still devouring what was left of her family. The hunter was a formidable warrior of a great reputation, and it would not be easy to defeat him. At one of your wise men's behest, your ancestors dug a great pit, lined it with punji stakes, and covered it. They then called out to him to come and join them for a feast. He came outside happily, his mouth still smeared with blood and gore.

"As they walked along the path, he began to suspect something and began to run! The others realized they had no choice but to push him into the pit. The hunter grabbed at one of them, and they both fell in screaming. It was a scene to chill the coldest killer's heart. As he was impaled upon the sharp bamboo spikes, the scent of the hunter's blood filled the air, and his screams of pain and rage instilled fear in every living thing that heard him that night. But the humans knew that they had to finish him off. It was too late for their friend who had fallen face first into the now blood-drenched stakes. They stabbed the hunter and hurled heavy stones onto his body until his hate-filled eyes stared back at them only in silence.

"Your people were mortified. Never before had anyone done this, and the terror that any one of them could do it shook them to the core. It was then they decided to lie, and they told the world that he had not gone mad, that he was not insane, but that a tiger had done it. That a tiger had disguised himself as the hunter and taken his place, because you could not admit to yourselves the awful truth of your own nature.

"Perhaps he could have been helped. But then again, perhaps not. In the West, the ancient Wolf Kings tell a similar tale of a young girl and her grandmother. And in the end, we all have seen your capacity for violence, no matter how you try to hide it. In London, they still whisper of the killer at East End. In France, Sir Gilles De Rais, who served by the side of Joan of Arc, is remembered more for his barbarous butchering of children than his valor. In America, who doesn't remember Dahmer, Gacy, Speck, and Charles Francis Ng?

"For centuries afterward, you had no jails but merely pushed those who had done wrong into the jungles, waiting for my people to take them, to eat them. You were ever afraid that their fiendish spirits would return as five-toed tigers, determined to drag the innocent with them into our kingdom of shadows. We did you a favor. We took them and tore them apart, and you repaid us by hunting us to near-extinction at the first chance you got. Human gratitude. Such a marvelous thing.

"You can keep your killers, now. But when my people are gone from this world, and you have no one to feed them to, what will happen? I wonder." The Tiger King smiles cruelly. He steps forward and with a single sharp claw cuts a gash into my arm. As the scent of my own blood reaches my nose, I hear him say, "Something to remember this by, to let you know that all this was real.

"Take this tale to your people, Storyteller. Now that we tigers can cause you no fear, the only thing we can give you is the truth. But I doubt it will help you sleep any better at night . . ."

With those words, the Tiger King gives a tremendous roar that shakes the entire room, a roar filled with laughter and sadness, a regal beast resigned to his kingdom's end. The Tiger King's roar is soon joined by a hundred, a thousand grotesque voices gibbering, hissing, weeping, and snarling, fading away in half-hearted protest like an exhausted secret army of mad phantoms ordered to march back to the dark pits of a distant hell. The feral eyes on the walls seem to turn to blood and yellow bile, dribbling down to the floor and flowing between the aging floorboards.

I watch silently as the once great Tiger King himself crumbles apart into so many broken shadows that slither away beyond sight. My captor who held me for so long sniffs once behind my ears and releases me, gone without another sound.

Soon, the last of the Tiger King's entire court has returned to the darkness, and I am left alone, my arm bleeding, a small stack of blank paper before me.

I hear a low voice growl from the shadows. "Now, write."

Outside, a blackbird laughs.

⁑ ⁑ ⁑

The Last War Poem

I tell you, this is the last word for this war.
This little side war we were the center of.
There is no justice from poetry—
Any veteran can tell you that.
They want their land, their lives,
Their livestock back.
Grenade fishing in the aftermath of Phou Pha Thi
Has lost its novelty
To the man with a bullet fragment rattling
In his body, slowly tearing him apart.
Write, they tell me.
Write what?
We lost, we were forgotten, we are ghosts.

We are victims of fat tigers and foreign policy.
There is no Valhalla, only memories of Spectre gunships
There is no Elysium, only pleas for asylum.
This jungle is filthy.
There was shit. There was blood.
There were refugees
Who to this day cannot explain why they were the enemy
When the Communists came.
Their sons fought. Their brothers died.
Their uncles, maimed, were hauled screaming into the shadows
    of the PDJ.
Write, they tell me, so people won't forget.
So someone will know.
Lift their broken bodies with my words, bring them out
And say we did not die in vain.
For every bullet hole,
Let there be a sonnet to stitch the truth back together.
For every eye gone blind,
Let there be something to take its place.
Something.
Anything.
How can you not have words for the war of whispers?
How can you not shout, now that the whispering is done?

And I swear, each time I break this promise, that the next time
Will be the last word I write about this damn war.

╫   ╫   ╫

Fury

And I swear sometimes
I'm going to take this town down
Downtown
Around town like a London Bridge
And a Korean song.
Gonna grab my shabby gear
And pull down a titan's ear.
Gonna holler till the walls buckle
Yawping and squawking
Whatever a man's gotta do
To get through to you.
The revolution is actually
A straight line to change
You can't keep going in circles—I see that now.
He's left, she's right. Who's wrong?
That's not even the question.
You see, we're free.
To Be in an age of empty
Is like a period at the end
Of a one-word sentence.
I got fire at the bottom of my shoes
Like I scraped myself on a dragon.
I've got a body of mud
That's tired of being treated like dirt.
I got water flowing for a heart
'Cause oceans, oceans always get the last word . . .
And I swear sometimes
This town ain't gonna take me down.

Wisdom

I

The Greeks say wisdom begins
with a face in the mirror that
says I do not know.

Sun Tzu needed a lovely girl's head to show
that knowing yourself
and knowing your foe
was enough to win a war best won without
a single drop of blood upon these rosy roads
filled with beauty.

Confucius with his aging pupils
had enough time to scribble out
"It is only the wisest and the very stupidest who
    cannot change."

The lousy old man from Ho-nan in his laid-back way says,
"Between good and evil, how much difference?"

On the Internet, I can find a copy of the I Ching
that will give free readings at the click of a button
(if I'm too lazy to toss the coins and yarrow)
with all of the reliability of a tarot deck stripped
of the minor arcana.

Exacting physicists say that
everything that rises must converge
and every action carries an opposite reaction
equal and pure.

The Zen monks in the mountains think they can
get away with the "I don't know" of *fushiki* and
nothing more than an empty fist.
If they aren't careful it will cost all of them their lives.

The Chinese say that wisdom begins when you
begin calling things by their proper names.

An Amway rep (who shall remain anonymous)
says tough times don't last but tough people do and
it's best to go into business for yourself but not by yourself.
Such wisdom is as old as the pyramids. Depending on
      whom you talk to.

In some cultures,
it is rude to talk to someone if you have nothing to say,
but after a time you might find that saying nothing and
saying something amount to the same thing.

II
A Hmong man was quoted obscurely:
"The world is only as large as a man is willing to walk."

Exhausted and weary, the GIs in Kuwait say: "Wheels are
      better than heels."

Mortal Kombat between its savage rounds contends
there is no knowledge that is not power.
It's not worth
losing your head
or your heart
for a quarter.

From the lightless grave,
Lord Acton wags his ink-stained fingers powerlessly,
in disapproval
of abuse
and absolutes.

Thundering Mr. Eliot through an April haze
murmured incomprehensibly
with a lost Brahmin's lullaby:
Datta, Dayadhvam, Damyata;
while a shrieking young boy from the back streets
can only see
a wasted mile of indigo ink.
It will never be his mantra.

The dog whispers conspiratorially
"If you cannot kill it or eat it,
play with it or sleep with it, or even crap on it,
leave it alone."

But then again, they say dreaming dogs lie, don't they?

Huxley wishes that in sixty years he could have produced
a message more profound than "treat people a little more nicely,"
while the Beatles proclaim
that all you need is love

After all of this, a young mother looks at me and asks
"Why bother looking at all, if that's the best you can offer?"

Peering down into that cavernous cradle
and her trusting baby's lively smile,
How can I come empty-handed?

Va-Megn Thoj ✐

Hmoob Boy Meets Hmong Girl

FADE IN: INTERIOR—DANCE PARTY—NIGHT

The room is crowded with people dancing to blaring music. Tooj and Jennifer, the only two Hmong in the room, both in their mid-twenties, are on opposite sides of the dance floor, slightly swaying and nodding to the music, each with a cup of beer in hand. They scan the crowd. Finally, they see each other and briefly make eye contact. Tooj is obviously interested in Jennifer. Jennifer seems indifferent. After a little hesitation, Tooj makes his way across the dance floor to approach Jennifer.

> TOOJ
> Hey, good looking. Want to dance?

Jennifer either does not hear him over the music or she fakes not hearing.

> TOOJ *(much louder)*
> Hi!

> JENNIFER *(aloof, condescending)*
> Hi.

> TOOJ
> Cool party, huh? The music's pretty cool, very danceable.

Jennifer turns and moves a few steps away from him, annoyed. Tooj follows her.

> TOOJ *(losing confidence)*
> Do you want to dance?

Jennifer ignores him.

> TOOJ
> I thought since we're the only Hmoob at this party . . .

JENNIFER
What makes you think I'm Hmong?

TOOJ
Chances are if you're Asian around here, you're Hmoob.

JENNIFER
Even if I was, that doesn't mean I'd automatically dance
with you. I don't dance with—or date—Hmong men.

TOOJ
Whoa, your highness, excuse me.

JENNIFER
What did you call me?

TOOJ
Forget it! It's not worth it!

He begins to walk away.

JENNIFER
Whatever.

TOOJ *(turning around)*
You know what? You're a bitch! You're a clueless bitch!

JENNIFER
You know what? You're a jerk, just like every Hmong
man in America. You're arrogant, macho, conservative,
ignorant, and sexist. Don't you think I'm too old for
you? I'm not fourteen or fifteen, and I'm definitely not
a virgin! I'm impure! I'm used goods! Why don't you go
to Thailand in your little polyester suit, Mr. Big-Shot-
Hmong-from-America, and find yourself some illiterate
teenage girl who'd stay home and cook for you?

TOOJ

Whoa, Ms. Hmoob Feminist is having a bad day.
PMS, huh?

JENNIFER

Typical. I could see you coming a mile away, Hmong man.

TOOJ

That's right, you better get out of my way. I'm Hmoob
and proud of it. Unlike some people who don't even want
to acknowledge they're Hmoob. What kind of a name is
"Jennifer," anyway? Don't sound like Hmoob to me.

JENNIFER

Oh, and I guess just 'cause your name is *Tong,* you're
so Hmong, huh?

TOOJ

More Hmoob than you. And it's not *Tong.* It's Tooj.

JENNIFER

Okay, *Tooj,* what makes you such an expert on Hmong?

TOOJ

Because I know who I am.

JENNIFER

You think you know me better than I do myself?

TOOJ

I know your kind well enough.

JENNIFER

What kind is that, Mr. Hmong?

TOOJ

The kind that would change her Hmoob name
to Jennifer.

JENNIFER
Fuck off. You don't even know me.

TOOJ
I wouldn't want to know you.

JENNIFER
Oh, but I *so* want to know you.

TOOJ
You're just another wannabe. I'm surprised you haven't bleached your hair blonde and had your eyelids cut up.

JENNIFER
Why don't you teach me how to be a good Hmong woman? Teach me how to always walk behind a man, never shake hands with him, always let him eat at the table first, never have eye contact with him, and always defer to him.

TOOJ
Yes, Hmoob woman, serve me! That's all I want in a Hmoob woman. She is to only serve me and bear me a dozen children before she's twenty-five, hopefully all boys. At least she'll know she's Hmoob.

JENNIFER
Hmong man, you are my master. I'm just a lowly servant, bought and paid for. My life belongs to you.

TOOJ
I bet your last name isn't even Hmoob anymore. It's probably like Chuekiayong or something. What kind of a made-up crap last name is that?

JENNIFER

For your information, your Hmongness, my last name happens to be Lee.

TOOJ

Oh.

(pause)

I'm a Lee, too. Well, guess there's no point in us talking anymore since we're both Lees. See you around.

JENNIFER

Jerk.

They give each other disgusted looks and go their separate ways.

FADE OUT.

Ka Vang ∽

REM & Dab & Neeg & Dab Neeg

Author's Note *This poem is inspired by a Hmong folktale about a Tiger-Monster who kills a Hmong father and assumes his identity so he can eat the man's family. The Tiger-Monster devours the entire family except for the youngest daughter, Yer. She outwits him and later slays the Tiger-Monster.*

Inside,
my interior
not on the exterior
I wait for Yer
floating in a chasm
between REM, the *Dab,* the *Neeg,* the *Dab Neeg*
lurking underneath the humid green canopy
my layers, yellow and black
stripes
cover my
outside
like a snug fur jacket
inside,
patiently in my disguise
I wait for Yer
opium swirls my mind
drip—drip—drip
silence engulfs time
roaring hunger pains
stretch my inside
ripple through my spine
I sharpen my fangs and claws on a fibula
watching ants drill holes
in-out, in-out, in-out
of rotting flesh

drip—drip—drip
into a pool
BLOOD
flesh, torn asunder,
fanned across the bamboo hut
from an impolite serial killer without
table manners
I lick my victims with pride
which
I hide
as I wait for Yer,
little girl
on the exterior
soon she'll be in my interior
underneath a mask, I hide
and ask with a lie
"Yer, come down. Your father is hungry!"

ෆ ෆ ෆ

Twinkies

Paint your face red, white, and blue
Decorate your eyes with stars and
Stripes
Insert color contacts until it gives you
Cataracts
Bleach your black hair blonde
Don't forget the roots
You'll never wash your skin white
Consider yourself a Twinkie
Yellow on the outside—
Tasteful.
In between—
White fluff.

෴ ෴ ෴

Extraordinary Hmong

I am the extraordinary Hmong
rice-paddy eyes
mouth full-open, filled with opium poppy seeds
hair long, black, like the Mekong
the ghost of my ancestors swimming on my back
waves breaking my spine—
sinking like silver
clapping with the poetry of *Kwv Txhiaj* to the murky
    depth of my
sunburnt-yellow buttock

crisped by the ungrateful McDonald-eating sun as I slave
    beneath him
I am not sushi
I am not take-out
I do not have an ancient secret
Pillsbury Dough people do NOT ask me for the
    Dalai Lama's number
karate chops do not regulate my hands
and the monks from Shaolin Temple are revolting
I do not know Jet Li
only jet lag when my spirit crosses the ocean to be delivered
    to Toys-R-Us
but Hmong-R-Not
welcome
in country clubs,
in corporations,
inside,
janitors, short-order cooks, and factory workers
please apply
wax yourself on, wax yourself off
I already jack off
so don't Daniel-san me
I am nobody's son
a nomad
sowing my seeds, riding my *plig*
straight into your fortune cookie
carrying more wisdom in my pockets than Plato's
    philosopher king
driving down University Avenue
my future coming through the rearview
Shee Yee riding steady on his steed

pounding drums
snapping *Qeej*
clinking gongs
and ancestors' howls
fill my ears
with silent sounds of pride
it says
I am the extraordinary Hmong

ෆ ෆ ෆ

Yellow Man's Burden

We built your railroads
In the Old West
Dug your diamond mines
In India
Harvested your rubber trees
In Vietnam
Fought your war
In Laos
Carried you on our backs
In China
Yet you call us a burden
SAVAGES
Animals to be civilized
Taught to
Worship your God
Eat with your forks and spoons
While you rape and plunder our land
To build your armies

So you could rape and plunder
Our land
Made to hate the color of our skin
And neglect our ancestors
You made us docile
Fetuses trapped in a white womb
Emasculate our men
Trade our women for cigarettes
Good in math
Bad drivers
Laundromat owners
Kung fu experts
Second-class citizens
Hey! Rudyard Kipling
Here's an answer for a question you never asked:
You are the burden we must overcome
The Yellow Man's burden.

෬ ෬ ෬

Ms. Pac-Man Ruined My Gang Life

Mandy stole my boyfriend, Tiny. The RCB, or the Red Cambodian Bloods, called him "Tiny" because he stood at six feet with iron arms. He was big for a Khmer. Everyone respected him because of his size, except me. I didn't like Tiny because, well, he was tiny, about the length of a fortune cookie and as thick as a Bic pen.

A Puerto Rican mama, Mandy had yellow fever. Every three months, an Asian brother passed her to another like a coat that had been worn but lost its appeal. She met up with Tiny at a party that I didn't attend because I was working. Within minutes Mandy was wrapped around Tiny tighter than a bun around a hot dog.

Being dumped didn't bother me at all. Well, maybe just a bit. But Tiny was no trophy to be fought over. He didn't care that his father was killed in a Khmer Rouge labor camp because he wore glasses, or that his mother was raped by boys his age when Pol Pot's people came to his village. The killing fields were the streets of south Minneapolis for him. Tiny was only interested in getting high and getting laid, and it didn't have to be in that order.

But, when you live the life of a gangsta girl, a woman stealing your man, particularly if she was from a rival gang, was a major sign of DISRESPECT, and therefore a serious justification for war.

"What about your rep?" my home girls implored, trying to convince me to jump Mandy. "Gurl, if I waz you, I'd cap her ass."

"It ain't like that," I replied, pushing down a hand made up into the sign of a gun.

It had been awhile since our last gang fight and now my girls were itching to do damage. Mandy suddenly emerged as a convenient target. Last night, we jumped two black girls for cutting us off on University Avenue. Like a scene out of a bad seventies car flick, we chased them down, trying to run them off the road until they pulled over somewhere between Snelling and Vandalia. Getting out of their beat-up Oldsmobile, they reminded me of Aunt Jemimas, huge with rolling fat. But there were five of us and only two of them.

Nikki, my best friend, did a pretend karate kick she saw in a movie just to scare them as we approached cursing and threatening. She loves to perpetuate the myth that all Asians know kung fu. We jumped on them with our brass knuckles and razor blades and left them bleeding by the side of the road.

"I don't want to throw down, at least not for him," I told

Nikki as we sat on my bedroom floor. "His father was killed by Pol Pot's regime, and he thinks that stands for a specialized Khmer joint!"

"Cindy, you are the only one who cares about this shit," said Nikki, twisting her head in a circle. "Besides, you're Hmong, not Khmer, so why the fuck do you care? This is St. Paul, not Southeast Asia. Think about the now, the hea! You can't let any ol' hole steal your MAN!"

Her fingers were in my face, accusing me of not protecting my property, our property. She made it clear that we would go to war. In a way, being in a gang is a lot like being in a democracy: the majority is right even when it becomes tyrannical.

"All right! Tonight at Louis's Billiards, her ass is grass!" I screamed, surprised by the hardness in my voice. Already my heart was hardening and my emotions evaporating so I could bring myself to hurt someone, to even take a life.

We called our homeboys and told them we needed back-up. About five of us gathered at my house in the late afternoon and started to plan our war strategy. We brought every scissors, hammer, screwdriver, nail, and tool we found in our fathers' toolboxes and wrapped them in duct tape so our fingerprints wouldn't be on the weapons if the cops ever got a hold of them.

Next we put tape on the gun, the one gun we all shared, which I was still holding from the last time we shot a Laotian girl for looking at Nikki the wrong way.

Sam, our backer who had a beef with Tiny's gang, picked us up at seven and took us to a gas station where we changed ten dollars into quarters and divided them among the five of us. The change came in handy if the cops came and we had to flee the scene on foot. That way, we could call home base, Sam's celli, from a gas station to be picked up. We had partners to run with just in case someone was shot or needed help. It wasn't the invasion of Normandy, but it was a scheme that worked. My only concern was that Louis's was located on a hill and it was January in Minnesota. The snow and ice was the unseen enemy.

We got to Louis's before Mandy and Tiny. I didn't see fear in my girls, and they didn't see fear in me. But my right toe, covered beneath the thick sock, twitched from anxiety at the thought of breaking open a head like a coconut with my bare hands. Only one part, an unseen part feared. My mouth was foul and my soul had enough hate to turn a man into stone like Medusa, but this was reality and not a myth.

I played my favorite old-school video game, Ms. Pac-Man, to shake off any doubts. I pretended the ghost was Mandy and Tiny, and I was chomping them up to be stronger. Chomping away, first the cherries, then the strawberry, then the banana, which meant I reached the highest level of the game.

"Damn!"

"Whussup, second thoughts?"

"No. This is my highest score, and I'm dead. Hey, can you spare me a quarter?"

"But the quarters are for—"

"Now, three-two-one! Nikki, please! I need that quarter. I've got to beat this game."

She hesitantly handed me a quarter. Thirty seconds later she handed me another quarter, and another.

"That's enuff, gurl! You should be keeping an eye on the door unless you want Mandy to come in hea and blow your brains into the machine. Your back is towards the door!"

"Thought you got my back?"

The clicking sounds of billiard balls hitting each other and rolling to the pockets faded into the darkness when Mandy and Tiny arrived with some of Tiny's gang members.

He took one look at me and motioned his crew to exit. They were gone and there would be no fight. I turned back to the machine, back to defeating Ms. Pac-Man, a truly worthy opponent.

But it wasn't over for my friends. They crowded around me with their smeared lipstick mouths yapping at me to pursue Mandy and Tiny. Like a mindless zombie I headed toward the door. My hands slipped into my jeans pocket for the scissors. Walking into the cold St. Paul night from the musky billiard hall, my excited breath formed a line of smoke from my mouth to the dry sky. Mandy and Tiny were about to get into their car when I screamed their names.

"Come over here!"

Tiny walked toward me like John Travolta in *Saturday Night Fever.* Mandy followed closely behind.

"Is Mandy your new girl?"

"Yeah," he said in his typical slow drawl.

"Why'd you dump me?"

"'Cos."

"'Cause what?"

"'Cos you're a crazy hole. Woman, I don't want no girl who's gonna get in my face, riding my ass about getting a job, fighting for my rights as a color man. I just don't care 'cos I just wanna have fun. And lately, you haven't been fun. You changed . . ."

It was about the sex. For men, it's always about the G-thang. I knew I should have placed more of a priority on that, but I really didn't care for it.

My home girls urged me in Hmong to hit Mandy and they would follow. One of Tiny's hangers-on, Joe, got all tough and stepped up.

"Why yo bitches in my boy's face?"

"This is between the girls," said Sam, who cocked the gun in his pocket loudly.

"Yo, like you said, um, it's between the girls," replied a frightened Joe.

Nikki got tired of the rhetoric and took out a screwdriver from her pocket. She stabbed Mandy in the chest. Mandy let out a howl as Nikki drilled it into her coat and deeper. The next moments happened so fast that it is hard to explain all the details. I followed Nikki's lead and thrust the scissors into Mandy's stomach. The other girls hammered Mandy with their fists and weapons. But she was tough. Her hard fist slammed into my face and back. We were like bees attacking her, and she was swatting us off.

I stopped and saw Tiny's worried face. He was too selfish to truly care for Mandy, but he didn't like an unfair fight. Tiny couldn't lift a finger to help Mandy for fear of Sam shooting him and his homies. But I still don't think he would have interfered even if he had a gun. He couldn't risk going to war with Sam, at least not over a woman.

I tried yanking the scissors out of Mandy, but it was caught in something, maybe her coat, or skin? After three or four tries, I managed to pull it out and slashed her across the face.

Mandy lay on the ground moaning in agony. A circle of blood formed on the snow underneath her head like an unholy halo. We took turns kicking Mandy until we heard police sirens in the distance.

"Let's go!" Nikki said.

We dropped our weapons and scattered. My partner Nikki and I started running down the hill into an unlit alley along University Avenue. I slipped and rolled, twisting my ankle. Pain shot through my leg as I tried to stand up. Limping down through the alley, I couldn't keep up with Nikki.

"Whassup with your foot?"

"Sprained ankle," I huffed.

The sirens got closer. The Five-O must have seen us run into the alley.

"Into the garbage bin before it's too late," she said.

Nikki, who was more athletic, pushed me into a dumpster behind a Vietnamese restaurant on University Avenue. My face landed on a pile of old chicken lo mein. It would be three years before I could eat lo mein again. The dumpster reeked with the rudest, most obnoxious odor, which penetrated my clothes, hair, and skin. Nikki jumped in and crawled to the other side.

The siren came closer, but as the squad car approached it was turned off. We heard the wheels of the car on the snow. Silently and slowly it stalked us. I expected the lid of the bin to open and blinding lights from a flashlight to shine on my face. My parents would be disappointed with me again when they came to pick me up from juvenile hall. My mother would cry and my father would threaten to kill me. Then it dawned on me that I had just turned eighteen, so I wouldn't get off so easy. I had forgotten about my birthday, which raised the stakes.

We waited in the bin for hours, not saying a word. Not even when I felt a million small and slimy creatures crawling up my arms. After a while I could make out Nikki's large watery eyes in the dark. Then I saw her doing the same thing I was, slowly picking the maggots off of her body. My right ankle throbbed with pain, but I couldn't move to rub it, worried that I would give away our hiding place.

Were the police waiting for us to emerge like filthy pigs from the pen? Maybe they wanted to play a joke on us, and the entire gang strike force was waiting for us to appear.

But there were no lights, no handcuffs, and no police dogs, only our shadows as we climbed out of the garbage bin.

I vomited all the way to the nearest gas station. We found a pay phone, but it was broken, so we walked to another station about a half-mile away. Afraid that the cops were still looking for us, we hid in doorways as cars drove by. The ice and cold made it difficult for the both of us to move faster.

"I think gangs have it easier in Cali," I said, trying to make light of our situation. Nikki was not amused. I wondered if Mandy was dead. Would Tiny still find her pretty with that scar I made on her left cheek?

Nikki was becoming increasingly frustrated and took out a pack of smokes. I knew she thought I had let my home girls down by my unwillingness to jump Mandy. I had become useless.

She took out a cig and placed it in her mouth without lighting it up. She was trying to quit.

When we got to the second pay phone, we realized we were out of quarters.

"Where are they?" she screamed.

"In the Ms. Pac-Man game."

"Cindy? Why did you do that? How will we reach Sam now!"

"I forgot. I had a good game," I said defensively. "Look, I never told you to give me all of your quarters!"

Reeking like a bad Vietnamese restaurant, with my ankle sprained, I knew it was the last gang fight for me. I had turned eighteen and would no longer get a slap on the hand if I were caught. Tiny was right, my interests had changed. But more importantly, I had changed. The role of being a gangsta girl was becoming too narrow for all that I wanted to do with my life. Even if Tiny didn't care about his future, I did about mine.

"I think this is it for me," I turned to Nikki and said.

Somehow she wasn't surprised.

"It's about time. I always knew you didn't have it in you. I wondered how long you'd last. I've got a bad habit that I'm also trying to quit so I understand, but the others won't."

"I can take care of myself."

"I've got your back."

She pulled out a paper clip from her pocket, and I started to laugh. The paper clip method was an old-school way to trigger the phone into thinking a quarter was put in. Of course, it no longer works on these new pay phones with the calling card feature. We called Sam to come and pick us up.

A week later my girls and I met in a school parking lot where they beat me to a pulp. It was a small price to pay for getting out of a gang.

Disconnect

A ONE-ROOM APARTMENT—THE PRESENT

Curtain opens. The stage is black and a strong light shines on a young Hmong woman in the process of coloring her black hair blonde. She is humming a popular American tune. There is a telephone next to her. The phone rings, and she picks it up after the third ring.

KA
Hello?

VOICE (*Woman*)
Will you accept a collect call from the city of Long Cheng—
Pause.
Long Cheng?

KA
Sorry. Don't know anyone by that name.

Hangs up: CLICK. *Ka hums the same song and continues to color her hair. Phone rings. Ka waits until the third ring and picks up the phone.*

KA
Hello?

VOICE (*Man*)
Ka, this is GOD. Why did you hang up on Long Cheng?

KA
God, no thanks. Don't need any faith here.

Hangs up: CLICK. *The phone rings again. She picks it up immediately.*

KA
What! I am trying to dye my hair. I can't do that with you bothering me.

VOICE *(A man's voice, smooth and relaxing)*
Is the head of the household home?

KA
Yes, this is she.

VOICE
Good evening?

KA
Who's this?

VOICE
I am calling from the research firm of McDonald,
McBeth and McMoney. And we would like to take a few
minutes tonight and ask you a few quick questions,
which will help us market Mc-ism to people of other
cultures.

KA
Sure, that's important.

Continues to color her hair. BEEP—BEEP—BEEP *is heard from phone.*

Wait, someone is on the other line. Hold on, please.

Switches lines: CLICK.

VOICE *(A haunting blend of many people—like the
Borg Collective)*
Ka, we are the spirit of your Vang and Her ancestors. We
swam to Australia, dug the farmlands of French Guyana,
and even rode the elevator up the Eiffel Tower searching
for you. Our journey is almost over now that we have
found you. We must tell you—

KA
Stop! I can't talk right now. I have someone very
important on the other line. Bon voyage.

Switches lines again—CLICK—and continues to color hair.

KA

Sorry about that. It was just the 4,000-year-old spirit
of my dead ancestors.

VOICE

As I was saying, Ms.—?

KA

Vang, Cindy Vang, like the youngest one in curls from
The Brady Bunch. People have a hard time pronouncing
my real name, sounds too ethnic.

VOICE

Vang. How do you spell that?

KA

F-U-C-K.

VOICE

F-U-C-K. Speaking of ethnicity, what is yours?

KA

Hmong.

VOICE

What does Hmong mean?

KA

Slave.

VOICE

But your English is so good?

KA

Thanks. I know.

VOICE

Next question, where were you born?

KA
Laos.

VOICE
City?

KA
Um, I forget. I think it was a military base called
Lin Tieng or Lou Chue.

VOICE
Did you swim across the Mekong River?

KA
No. I flew over it on a C-130. No one swam across the
Mekong. This is just some Western Judeo-Christian
propaganda, a myth someone made up so we could feel
connected to white people, like Moses and his chosen
people crossing the Red Sea.

VOICE
If this is true, then why haven't you exposed it?

KA
Works for me.

VOICE
I am going to ask you two questions, which you can
answer true or false.

KA
True or false.

VOICE
Yes. The Hmong have eighteen clans.

KA
You mean plans. There is no vision for the Hmong
in the future.

VOICE

Good. Sixty-six percent of Hmong households live below the federal poverty level.

KA

Does that mean they don't get MTV?

VOICE

True or false?

KA

False. Everyone has MTV.

VOICE

What is the best way to assimilate the Hmong into the dominant culture? A: lose their language; B—

KA

CoCo Lee.

VOICE

What? Who?

KA

CoCo Lee. She's my favorite singer, but they don't play her on MTV. I wonder why? She's like an Asian Britney Spears, but without the big boobs.

VOICE

You've got great taste in music.

KA

I know.

VOICE

What is the best way to assimilate the Hmong into the dominant culture? A: lose their language; B: marry outside their race, C: lose their religion; D: all of the above; or E: none of the above?

BEEP—BEEP—BEEP

KA
Damn! I can't get these people to get off my back. E.
For sure, it's E: none of the above. The Hmong are
indestructible.

BEEP—BEEP—BEEP

Excuse me again; I have to see who is on the other line.

VOICE
No problem. Time is on my side.

Switches lines: CLICK.

KA
Who's this?

VOICE *(A young girl)*
Ka, this is your future. I have come back in time to
warn you that—

KA
Ebenezer Scrooge is not home!

Switches lines: CLICK.

VOICE
That was quick. Who was that?

KA
Oh—just someone who thinks it's Christmas.

BEEP—BEEP—BEEP

Hold on again.

Switches lines: CLICK.

VOICE (*Young girl*)
Don't hang up!

KA
Why not?

VOICE
Because the past, present, and future have decided—

KA
I don't know any of these people. I do know Clotho,
Lachesis, and Atropos. I brought one of their designer
dresses last week. You have the wrong phone number.

Moves her hands to switch lines.

VOICE
Wait! We need to warn you about the future. There are
signs that can't be ignore—

KA
My forecast said it's going to be clear and sunny.

Switches lines: CLICK.

Sorry about that. I understand the importance of good
research and marketing information, and I really want
to help you.

VOICE (*Relaxing and smooth*)
You must be a popular woman with so many calls
on a Friday night?

KA
Yes, it's hard when everyone wants a piece of you.

VOICE
Your spirit must be scattered?

KA
No, not at all.

VOICE
McDonald, McBeth and McMoney would like to thank
you for your loyalty. I have few more questions, then
we'll be done.

KA
That's okay. I don't mind answering your questions.
I can talk to you while coloring my hair.

VOICE
Good . . . good. I am sure you are using one of our
products.

KA *(Loudly)*
It's the best!

VOICE
Great. How do you color hair?

KA
First, I use bleach to strip all the black from my hair
until it turns white. Then I cover it with blonde dye.

VOICE
Sounds complicated.

KA
No. It's quite simple.

VOICE
Does the bleach burn your skin?

KA
No. It feels good, like lotion.

VOICE
Back to the survey, what are the best qualities of the
Hmong?

KA
Pause.
Men can have as many wives as they want . . .
Pause.
Oh, we've been on TV lately. The Hmong have gotten
a lot of publicity. A beautiful young woman killed her
seven kids while they played hide and seek. Let's see,
we can also get marry as early as we want.
Begins to laugh.

VOICE
What's so funny?

KA
Nothing.

VOICE
What's so funny?

KA
I hate to talk about negative things in my community,
but . . .
Pause.
. . . when I was in the seventh grade, I met a classmate
who married a man twice her age.

VOICE
How old was she?

KA
Twelve.

VOICE
Twelve?

KA

Twelve. She was sick every day in homeroom and finally
I asked her why. She told me her husband demanded a
hand job, a blowjob, and one whole minute of sex before
he came.

VOICE

Hmong men must be bulls.

KA

Mooooo—more like cows. You see . . .
Pause.
. . . she hadn't had her period, so the nightly fuckings
were messing her insides up.

They both laugh.

VOICE

Do you think you will marry a Hmong man?

KA

Almost did once!

VOICE

Was he a bull or a cow?

KA

Actually a dork. A grade-A dork.

VOICE

Really?

KA

I was like thirteen when my parents forced me to
marry my second cousin from California. He wanted
me for his second wife. Yuck! I didn't want to marry
him because I wanted to go to college, have a career,

and marry someone like Brad Pitt. My parents beat
me badly so I ran away from home.
Laughs.

VOICE
Are you home now?

KA
Home is where the hair, I mean heart is.

VOICE
After using our products, are you a satisfied customer?

KA *(Loudly)*
It's the best!

VOICE
Then as a preferred customer would you recommend
our products to other Hmong?

KA
Certainly. If they don't already have it.

VOICE
Can you give me the names of family and friends who
would want to try our products and take the survey?

KA
I sure can. Say, you have a fun job meeting new people
and asking questions. Do you think I can get a job like
yours?

VOICE
I am glad you brought that up. In fact, we are currently
taking applications at our Glass Ceiling headquarters for
entry-level jobs. It's perfect for a career woman like you.

KA
Where do I sign up?

BEEP—BEEP—BEEP

VOICE
Are you going to get that?

KA
Naw. It is probably just a stranger selling me something useless. Now where were we? Oh yeah, where do I sign up for the job?

VOICE *(Speaking fast)*
We have now come to the demographic portion of our survey.

KA
Yee-haw. I'm a real patriot!

BEEP—BEEP—BEEP

Though I've never cut down a cherry tree.

VOICE
Then what did you cut down?

KA
Bamboo. Thousands of bamboos in green tropical forests. I mean, you have to do something to pass the time when you visit your homeland.

VOICE
What is the highest level of education you have obtained: high school, undergraduate degree, or graduate degree?

KA
Vo-tech.

VOICE
Vo-what?

KA

Tech. Vo-tech. I took one year of secretarial classes
and one year of woodwork.

VOICE

Does this mean you are a secretary for a carpenter?

KA

Laughs.
No. I'm a waitress at Café Late.

VOICE

You mean Café Latté.

KA

No. Café Late. Someone forgot to tell the owner that
Latté has two *t*s. *C'est la vie.*

VOICE

Jeez, I wonder who did that?

KA

Actually it was *moi.* My French is somewhat rusty.
It's not exactly "Tree Bien." I first learned the language
of love in high school.

VOICE *(French accent)*
Au contraire. Votre Français c'est tres bien!

KA

Ahh, yeah, sure. I learned it from my French teacher.
La Teacher took me behind the stadium bleachers to
show me how good he was with his foreign tongue.

VOICE

You must be special to get all that personal attention
from such an important man.

KA

Moi? I guess I am "Tree Bien!" Did I tell you that I also speak Spanish? *Sí.* El grande taco with rancho salsa. German. Das sauerkraut, Das wiener, Das guten tag.

VOICE

Natürlich, Sie sprechen gut Deutsch.

KA

What? I don't speak Dutch, only German.

VOICE

Ja. Do you rent or own?

KA

I rent. I live above Café Late.

VOICE

That must be convenient.

KA

Yes. Oh yes it is.

BEEP—BEEP—BEEP

VOICE

What is your annual household income?

KA

Should I include tips?

VOICE

If you want.

KA

Forty.

VOICE

Forty thousand dollars a year.

135

KA

No, silly! Forty dollars a day. Tip not included.

BEEP—BEEP—BEEP

VOICE

How often do you go out? A: once a day; B: once a week; C: once a month; D: once a year.

KA

Pause.

None of the above.

Pauses, then laughs.

As you said, I am popular, but I really don't have time to go out between waitressing and learning French . . .

BEEP—BEEP—BEEP

VOICE

That's understandable. Are you going to get that?

KA

It's probably just the wrong number again.

VOICE

On a one-to-ten scale, where one is the lowest and ten is the highest, how would you rate being Hmong?

BEEP—BEEP—BEEP

KA

Ten! Definitely ten. I am so proud to be Hmong.

BEEP—BEEP—BEEP

I feel totally connected.

VOICE

Maybe you should disconnect that second line?

KA

Soon. Can you hold again? *(Annoyed)* I have got to tell these people to leave me alone once and for all.

Switches lines: CLICK.

Hello?

VOICES *(Long Cheng, God, Ancestors, and Future)*
We were told this is Ka Vang's number. Is this her?

KA
Pause.
I ... um ... am ... I ... um ...

Looks confused and drops the phone receiver: CLICK. *Dial tone sounds and light fades.*

THE END.

943

Chatter, footsteps, and the sound of doors slamming disturbed the relative quiet, as students of various sizes and colors rushed from another school day. The blue Honda door swung open, and Yer stepped out. She walked to the driver's side and finger-combed her hair, tucking a stray strand behind her ear. Leaning down, she planted a good-bye kiss on Kong.

"I'll see you tomorrow?" she asked.

Kong, a cigarette tucked between his teeth, gave her a lop-sided grin. He tilted his head slightly.

A smile appeared on Yer's face. "In front of the school, okay."

Kong watched her walking toward the buses parked in front of the school. Yer's behind swayed in perfect rhythm with her long, sleek hair. Long black hair he grabbed when it suited him. He imagined it wrapped around his middle—cascading over his body and tantalizing his nether regions.

Damn girl was driving him crazy! Three months and he hadn't gotten past third base. What the hell? He suggested they go to the Hi-Lo Motel, but that upset her. He even offered to take her home with him. That did not appease her, as it had the others—so many others. The girl pouted until he took her to the mall.

There was an exclusiveness that kept dragging Kong back to Yer, even though his senses told him it was time to move on. Something that he didn't understand. Oh, she loved him, but she was holding something back—a piece of her he couldn't capture. He was sure it was connected to that spell she wove with her hair.

They were four-plexes, standing next to each other like the three weird sisters. Large square buildings with small front lawns devoid of grass but abundant in yellow dandelion, crab-grass, and dirt. Looming over the entire street with large stone blocks painted white to hide age and wear. The middle building bore the weight of a sagging porch. Chipped paint fell like summer snowflakes. A cracked sidewalk led to an unlocked wooden door. No screen door.

943 Edmund Avenue, apartment 2. Two bedrooms, a combined living room and dining room, a tiny sunroom in the back, a kitchen, and one bathroom for nine people. Ten, if you counted Yer's father, which she did not. Her mother, two baby brothers, and Yer's father, Vang Cha, when he was there, shared the "master bedroom." With a bunk and a queen, it was difficult to squeeze a dresser drawer into the second bedroom, but somehow the family managed. Yer, with the privilege of being the eldest daughter, slept on the bottom bunk, while her younger sister May slept on the top one. Nou, the youngest daughter, shared a queen with her frail grandmother. The sunroom had been converted into a third bedroom, which Yer's older brother, Seng, shared with his new wife, Pa Houa.

Yer, Nou, and Pa Houa walked up the cracked sidewalk to the door. As they strode into the hallway and up the narrow stairs, the smell of urine and smoke permeated through the dimness and into their nostrils. Nou swung her backpack onto her left shoulder and stuffed her hands into her pocket. She pulled out a ring of keys her mother had proudly presented her two years ago. The keys jingled as she jammed one into the keyhole.

The weary door opened with a loud squeak. Seng and Vang Cha sat on a sagging sofa watching *DuckTales*. The three girls were surprised to see their father at the apartment. He was usually at Bao's house, his first residence, a block from Lake Phalen. His hot gaze caused Yer's body to burn. She detected a hard glint in his eyes. He clenched his jaws, and his muscles tensed. Her father was mad; then again, he was always mad. She didn't know why he even bothered to visit them. Whenever he was there, he repeatedly scolded her for being a bad daughter.

Yer didn't want to spare him another thought. She was going to go into her bedroom and admire Kong's gift. She couldn't wait to call Ma, her best friend, and brag about her new Hornets jacket. Ma was going to be so envious. Kong was the most generous boyfriend in the world. She didn't know why she had been mad at him earlier. He wasn't a jackass like her father! Her nostrils flared. She turned and began to walk to her room. A strong hand grabbed her shoulder and twisted her around.

"Where have you been?" asked Vang Cha in Hmong.

"What?" Yer asked in English.

"Where were you today, gangster?"

"Why do you have to call me a gangster? I am not a bad girl!" Yer shrugged off her father's grip.

"Shit!" Seng said. "I'm leaving, man. I am sick of this shit! I can't even watch TV in this fucking apartment."

The door slammed shut as he left.

"School," she finally answered.

Her father's hand flew out and slapped her face. Yer fell to the ground, and her backpack strap slipped out of her hand as her Hornets jacket slipped off one of her shoulders.

"Ow-w-w!"

"Don't lie to me, you little whore."

"I'm not. I went to school. Ask Nou."

"The school called and said you weren't there."

Yer's bottom lip quivered as her eyes wandered to the phone. Her hands were clutched to her right cheek, which was throbbing harder than her heart. Heat flooded the back of her eyes.

"I was at school. Grandmother can't speak English. How can she—"

Vang Cha's hand was raised in a fist as he approached her, his face contorted.

"Don't lie to me. Your stepmother went to La Crosse today to visit her mother. I came home so Grandmother could cook me lunch, and your school called."

She was silent. Yer's jaw stuck out. She had no excuse. He would kill her if he discovered her special trips with Kong while she should have been at school. Nou and Pa Houa went to their rooms. They blasted the radio, and hip-hop music competed with Vang Cha.

The cries of two babies, her younger siblings, turned Yer's eyes to the window. They lay on a blanket thrown on the scratched hardwood. Grandmother sat on her rattan stool with flower cloth appliqué work in her hands, trying to make use of the little light that made its way between the buildings and into the apartment. She set it aside and picked up the babies.

"Are you going to tell me, you female dog?"

Yer wasn't going to tell him anything, the fuckin' asshole.

"I'm your father. Do I have to beat it out of you?"

She didn't care. She didn't consider him to be her father. He came over occasionally. He shared her mother's bedroom and got her pregnant. He didn't buy the groceries or pay the rent. He didn't buy her clothing or soothe her at night when she was scared. The state paid the rent, and food stamps bought the rice stored in the garbage bin and the noodles on top of the refrigerator.

"I hate you," Yer whispered.

A foot connected with Yer's side and a hand was in her hair, then a kick and another. She couldn't breathe.

"Stop, Cha. What kind of family are we? Are we people or are we monsters?" asked Grandmother.

"I am a human being, but this whore would rather be a dog."

"If the world walked through that door," Grandmother pointed to the entrance with her crooked finger, "and saw the behavior of our house, what could we say to them? Our house will not be able to hold up our face to the world."

"Don't speak to me about how our house will lose face to the world. It is because of this whore that we will lose face."

"You cannot beat my granddaughter. When you married my

daughter, you promised to care of her, take me into your house, and respect me. I will not allow you to continue this."

"I am the man in this house. I have to watch my family's reputation. We have a standing in the community that we have to protect."

Vang Cha stomped around the room, gesturing in the air with his hands.

"You don't know anything; your family came from hill trash. You people don't know how good Hmong people behave. No wonder you produced such a granddaughter."

Grandmother did not respond to his last comment. She rocked a baby in each of her arms, trying to soothe them in the midst of the racket.

"Whore, have you been fucking around? You female dog. Tell me!" His eyes dilated.

Yer was a virgin. She had never slept with a guy. Kong wanted her, but she always said no. Yes, she had let him touch her— and her—, but she had never slept with him.

"Why can't you be more like Bao, huh? She goes to school. She brings home good grades. You're as old as she is: you should know just as well as her."

"I'm not Bao. I'll never be her!"

Vang Cha's chest heaved up and down. He stared at Yer's face, fury building in him.

"She never speaks to me in this disrespectful tone. She dresses cleanly. She's not a slut like you."

Why did father call her a bitch and a whore? He never called Bao those names, but then, Bao was the first wife's daughter and Yer was the second wife's.

Yer's head hurt as Vang Cha pulled her to the rattan stool by her long ebony tresses. She brought her hands up to her head and tried to lessen the strain.

"Stop it! Stop it!"

"Who were you with?"

Vang Cha huffed and puffed as he grabbed Grandmother's sewing bag. His eyes zeroed in on a shining metal object in the bag. He pulled it out and walked toward Yer.

Yer's eyes widened and her face grew ashen. This time he was going to kill her. She never thought he would, but as he approached her with the scissors, she knew this was her time. Yer should have agreed to go with Kong.

Vang Cha grabbed her hair again. With a few slashes, pounds fell away from Yer's head.

"You asshole."

She felt a fist in the mouth and a kick in the stomach. Her father was in a rage she had never seen before.

"I'll teach you to talk to me this way."

The front door opened. Yer's mother was home from another day of making Christmas wreaths.

"Old man, stop it. Why are you beating my Yer?" she cried in distress.

Yer's mother, Choua, dropped her things and knelt by her daughter's side.

"I will not allow you to beat her this hard."

"Get out of my way."

Then Vang Cha slapped Choua.

Father beat mother because of her. She heard her mother's weeping joined with Grandmother's cries. Their pain flew out the window into the streets.

"I was with Kong," she screamed. "I was with Kong."

Vang Cha beat Yer until she told him everything. She went to McDonald's in the morning. Then they went to the St. Paul Student Center where they played pool. Finally, they went to Rosedale Mall where they had lunch and shopped.

"Please . . ." she whimpered through swollen lips.

His hand was shaking as he brought it up to deal another blow. Vang Cha paused for a moment, stilling the tremor, and looked at his fist. His eyes glazed over, and he twisted his lips into a grimace. He continued to beat her with a broom. On her legs, on her back—Yer rolled up into a tight ball. He couldn't stop.

"I knew you were with a man, whore. Who are his parents? Give me his number."

Vang Cha was on the phone. He called Kong's house. Kong was twenty-two, and he worked second shift at Sea-Tech. He wouldn't be home, but his parents would. Vang Cha demanded that Kong come and get Yer. She was no longer his daughter.

It was 12:30 A.M. when a knock on the door penetrated Yer's senses. She sat on the sofa with her arms wrapped around her knees. Her eyes were puffy and her nose red. A blue blotch marred her cheek and others ran up and down her arms.

Kong stood at the door with two older men, his father and uncle. His hands were stuffed in his pockets.

Kong had come. Still dressed in his work clothes, he pulled out his hands to shake Yer's father's, revealing the grime beneath his fingernails. His eyes wandered over the drab furniture and focused on Yer. His gaze penetrated her like a stabbing knife. Yer was unusually quiet. Her head bowed down, crouching on the sofa, she lifted her arms to cover her head. His lips tightened.

Vang Cha welcomed them into his home. He gestured for them to sit down at the table. The old men discussed the situation. The main concern: how best to save face. Yer would go home with Kong tonight, and on Friday he would return with a marriage broker to negotiate the bride price. The wedding would be on Saturday. It was very simple.

Would Kong be angry because he was being forced to marry her? No, he had offered earlier. Would he expect her to—? He was sitting at the table with the other men. She needed to talk to him and hear the reassuring words he had spoken earlier. She could not approach the table, though. The elders would say she was disrespectful. She had to know her place, a woman's place.

She wanted to lift her head and look at him, but she didn't want him to see how ugly she was. He would be disgusted. Yer raised her hands to cover her face. Her fingers rubbed her throbbing temples and brushed against the spiky fuzz that now covered her scalp. Her hair was gone—cut off at the roots.

⚜ ⚜ ⚜

The Case of the Red Pens

BEEP.

Email   Tuesday, April 20, 1999
To: All Corporate Employees
From: Tracey Berg
Re: Red pens

The box of red pens in the supply closet is missing. The box of red pens was just ordered from OfficeMax to mark off incoming inventory. They were not checked out on the supply list. If you took these pens or know of their whereabouts, please contact Kelly Hill.

Remember to write down any items you remove from the supply closet on the form in the box outside.

What a joke. Red pens. You click the X, deleting the email from your inbox. You have more important work to do than worry about the red pens. Paul Bedard wants the reports on his desk next Friday. The books need to be closed for this year, and then there was that call from the state labor board. No wonder the company stock is at an all-time low.

Pick up the phone and call Darlene. 612-780-1937.

"Honey, I'm running a little late."

She says, "Okay, but don't forget to pick up the beef. I want to make roast for dinner."

You reassure her and hang up. Click.

Rather be watching golf on TV, or playing basketball at the gym with the guys. Instead, with the daughter and son in tow, you're driving up the interstate. At least there's no traffic. Darlene went to the hairdresser with her sister, Marsha, and is having lunch at the club with friends.

"It'll be good for them to spend time with you," she said. "Mark and Marie love going to your office."

The kids think it's a treat to go to Daddy's office. A drive into the city and, afterwards, always McDonald's. Wait till they're adults, with a briefcase in hand, dressed in a suit, a company cell phone making them accessible twenty hours a day, seven days a week.

This is what America's all about. This is why you went to school for seven years.

You park outside the building. The best parking spot downtown. At least it's Sunday, so you don't worry about the meter maid. Greet Bill at the door.

"Pretty braids in your hair, young lady," Bill says.

Marie breaks into a smile and reveals her jigsaw-puzzle teeth. Her hand comes up to caress the proud braid.

"Aw, that ain't nothing special. Mommy does it like that every day, Mr. Bill," says Mark.

"Oh you! They *are* nice. Mommy says they make me look like Pollyanna, and Mr. Bill says they're nice. Didn't you?"

Say, "Kids!"

Bill ruffles Mark's brown hair as you go to the elevator.

With your sleeves rolled back and jacket hanging on the back of your chair, you sit. Rub eyes. You are weary from looking at the black screen. The numbers all run together, but you have to find out who received a fifty-dollar advance last June. Hear giggles and running little feet outside your door.

Damn Lynn. You should have fired her sooner. The girl had the organization of a garbage can. You shuffle through your third set of payroll reports for the day. If you had only known better. Hindsight is great.

BEEP.

> Email   Monday, April 26, 1999
> To: All Corporate Employees
> From: Tracey Berg
> Re: Missing box of bank statements
>
> Rachel Markey left a box of statements from Bank of America in the open cubicle in Treasury. This morning the box is missing. It is very important that we find the statements. If you moved the box or have seen it please contact me at ext. 670.

You don't recall seeing any box. 10:30 A.M. Coffee-break time. Like clockwork, you put down anything you are working on; today it's the reports. Pass by the filing girls. Just like every day, they are talking a mile a minute about their boyfriends. Since starting at Bedard's Balls and Baskets, you have been able to make out their whole life stories from the snatches of conversation you overhear on the way to the break room. Walk into the break room. You take your official Bedard's Balls and Baskets mug and fill it with coffee. The steam carries the aroma to your nose. No sugar, no cream. You take it like a man. At least you like to think so, like the cowboys in the westerns you watch on the Night Owl movie.

"Hi," says the new girl in Payables.

You say, "Hi." Can't remember her name.

She asks, "How's your day, Mr. Callahan?"

Small talk, great. "Fine, just fine."

The conversation eventually fizzles, and the new girl turns away to fill up her mug. Thank God, you think. You hate those messy conversations that you have to bear just to be polite, when you have nothing to say to a person. Makes you feel uncomfortable. Wonder sometimes if it would be more polite to just walk away, pretending you hadn't heard any greeting. At least you would be nicer in your head, instead of thinking, "Go away."

BEEP.

Reminder 1:30 P.M. Monday, April 26, 1999
Call dentist to schedule appointment for Mark.

BEEP.

Email   Tuesday, April 27, 1999
To: All Corporate Employees
From: Tracey Berg
Re: Missing box of bank statements

The box was found. Thanks to all employees who took the time to look for the box.

You roll your shoulders and rub the back of your neck.

A knock at the door stops you from cracking your back. Look up from the computer screen.

"Jeff, how's the monthly earnings report coming along?"

Say, "Fine, just fine."

"Be sure to have it on my desk by Friday morning. Make enough copies to pass out at the VP meeting."

The cigarette is secured between your teeth. In your right hand is a lighter, and your left hand shields it from the rain. You really need one of these! Click, click. The flame bursts to life just long enough to light the cigarette. The alcove, which most of the smoking employees use on their break, is full. You are at the very edge, and drops of rain pelt your backside. Your fingers are cold, and you can see the wrinkles and patches of hair at your knuckles. At times like this, know that mother was right. Smoking is bad for you. At least it's not snowing and five degrees below zero. At those times you feel downright dumb.

"Yeah, I found it in the electrical room."

"How did the statements get there?"

"I have no idea."

Think, so that's where they were. What kind of person would hide statements in the electrical room? Maybe Lynn got mad when you fired her and hid some of the information you are looking for. Decide to search the department.

The report is due tomorrow, and you return to work at 8:00 P.M. to finish up. The kids want to come along. Despite your protest to Darlene, they are sitting on your office floor.

"Stop laughing!" cries Mark. His face is scrunched up so that it is difficult for you to make out his brown eyes between his chubby cheeks and thick brows.

Marie holds her middle as she doubles over.

About to tear out all of your brown hair, say, "Stop screaming, Mark."

"But Marie is laughing at me."

Say, "Marie, stop laughing at your brother."

The kids go to the break room for drinks. Finally, peace and quiet.

Put in your calendar a reminder to get a babysitter.

You are sitting in a large leather recliner. The remote is in one of your hands; a can of Bud is in the other. You casually change the channel. The weekend is yours. Your plans: some fishing, a few games on TV, and outright sleeping in the back yard underneath the sun.

BEEP.

Email   Wednesday, May 5, 1999
To: All Corporate Employees
From: John Bedard, CEO
Re: Security

Bedard's Balls and Baskets has been experiencing a security problem. Paperwork and other company property are missing; things are not found where they were left. All employees are instructed to put away all company paperwork and lock their productivity stations when they leave them. Violation of this new rule will be grounds for dismissal. This new rule is to protect any personal items you might have and for company security. It is to protect you from being the next target.

If you have any information on the culprit, please contact me. Your identity will remain confidential.

After dinner, you and the wife talk in the family room. The kids are upstairs in their beds.

" . . . pens, some family pictures, rubber bands—almost everything imaginable. Nothing's happened to anything of mine, but you can't be too careful. It's just a matter of time," you say.

"Seems to be a shame: you can't even trust your coworkers nowadays."

"The world's going to the dogs."

People are different today.

It's late, so you decide to turn in. You climb up the stairs and walk down the hall.

"Honey, can you check on the kids?"

You open the first door on your left. The room is dim, except for the faint glow from the night-light and a shaft of light from the open door. Mark is wrapped in a blanket. His little head lies on a Power Rangers pillowcase. His hand is wrapped around a teddy bear and the dimples in his elbow show. You notice a drawing on the nightstand. You move the red pen on top and pick it up. You're able to make out a stick-figure portrait of a family. You are carrying a briefcase, Marie has her doll, and Darlene is the one with a skirt on. You don't remember the last time you had a free moment to see one of the drawings that Darlene always puts on the refrigerator.

Mental Note: put in calendar a reminder to spend more time with the kids.

Mayli Vang

Dreams of a Forgotten Widow

When it rains, I visit the earth and mud
Streets, the one-roomed houses
With their worn bamboo walls
And leaky roofs, families huddled
In corners during the monsoon season.

I see the plates of crusty rice and chicken
Left for ancestor spirits.
The smell of dirt and burning
Incense during meals of rice
And ginger root dipped in salt.

The toothbrush and comb
My husband kept, unused for fifteen years,
Hang on the side of the see-through
Wall. It rained. It rained.
It rained the day my husband left.

0 0 0

Some Old Hmong Woman

Some old Hmong woman
lives in the yellow high-rise
projects of North Minneapolis.
Each morning, she cracks
an egg in boiling water

adds salt and black pepper
to flavor. In the afternoon,
sitting on the faded blue
love seat, she eats Texas

oranges and licks her fingers.
Her eyes have become too bad
to *sawv paj ntaub*. In the evening,
she boils a store-bought chicken leg

in water, adds lemon grass to flavor.
At the small wooden table,
with the chicken leg and a bowl
of rice, she eats in silence.

Anthropologists have noted:
old people in the Eskimo culture
who became too feeble to contribute
to the family were left out in the snow

to die.

We Women
of the Hmong culture

We women of the Hmong culture
may now clean the plates
of what the men have left,
eat the remains while they pick
their teeth with wooden toothpicks.

They call this a privilege,
to be seated at the table
of those who were seated before.
To partake in this feast of remains

is a blessing beyond all measures.
Yet some she-witched women
"possessed by this newfound knowledge
of excessive freedom" are weary

of participating in such patriarchal
rituals of the old motherland.
They stare at the remains of half-eaten
meat—the imprints of a beloved uncle's

teeth still cut upon them—littered
among the cuisine grown cold
from hours of neglect.
Does no one wish to sit and taste?

The host and hostess invite
all us women to partake in the feast
of *laab*—ground beef,
half-cooked tendons—and chicken

boiled with withered herbs.
Biting our lips and our tongues,
we sit. With each bite into the feast
at hand, we remember

we are women.

0 0 0

Reflections of My Father

I was only four years old when my father died. We were living
in a refugee camp near the border of Thailand and Laos when
he decided to go back to Laos along with his stepbrothers. His
stepbrothers told him it was the noble thing for a son to do.
My mother tells me that he wanted to please his stepbrothers
and his mother, so he went along. On the way to Laos, he
stepped on a land mine and lost his leg. His stepbrothers left
him, still alive. He wouldn't have survived, they told us afterward, so instead of endangering their own lives by staying with
him or carrying him with them, they left him. We heard rumors
of his death weeks after my father had left on his journey, but
we didn't believe them until my uncles came back without him.

My father has been gone for more than twenty years, yet
recently I have written numerous essays about his death. I have
never been honest about him, always recounting more details
than I really know, my way of reassuring myself that I did know
him and that he did exist. The most immense fear I have carried
with me for as long as I can remember is the fear that I do not
know my own father. This fear lingers in my life because it
undeniably displays the fact that I cannot know myself if I do
not know my own father.

I often wonder what thoughts went through my father's head after he stepped on the land mine, lost his leg, and was lying on the dirt. No matter how great his pain was, my father never forgot his family. He made his stepbrothers swear to him that they would take care of us and threatened to come back and haunt them if they didn't. He must have lain there for days with agonizing pain. Maybe the pain of losing his leg was a comfort because it kept him from thinking about us, his family, and how his death would leave us orphaned and unprotected. His last hours must have been full of misery, thinking about his loved ones. He probably cursed the heavens for making his life one misfortune after another, but he must have prayed for our happiness.

All I have left of my father is his worn-out, faded yellow shirt and a black-and-white wallet-sized picture of him, taken when he was in his early forties. He looks younger, as if he was in his late twenties. In the picture his eyes seem sad but hopeful. He had so much to live for! His shirt hangs in the back of my closet. Sometimes when I cry, I wipe my tears on it, as if this shirt is a link between my father and me. Through this action, I imagine he will know my pain. I have tried sniffing my father's shirt, hoping to trigger a memory with a scent, but now there are only the smells of mothballs and paint. My father's shirt still hangs in my closet after all these years.

My mother often mentions my father to us. She says he was a shy man. There was no courtship when they got married because he was too shy. He saw my mother, fell in love, and came back a few weeks later to marry her. She didn't even know who he was until after the wedding when they were walking back to his village. When he spoke to her, he said simply, "Stop here. We're eating lunch." Not very romantic, but my father was a very serious, quiet, and reserved man. He wasn't the talkative type; instead, his words were important to him. When he said something, he meant it. Growing up abandoned by his father, who died when he was two years old, and his mother, who left him and his brothers when she remarried, my father must have learned the virtue of silence.

The circumstances of my father's death lead me to conclude that he wanted to be someone he wasn't. He wanted to be a hero. He always had to prove that he was the better person. That was his fatal flaw. He was always trying to please others and never for a moment thinking of himself. He helped others no matter what dangers were in it for him. He was too sacrificing, giving, kind, and humble. That's why he died: he was trying to right every wrong. No matter that his mother had rejected him: he was determined to earn her love and to prove to her that he was worthy of it. He was going to forgive her and love her if she asked. His mother probably asked him to return because she knew that she could easily manipulate him. He was a forgiving man; how could he refuse his own mother's request?

My attempts to recall any memories of my father have been futile. It couldn't be because I was too young; I remember being chased by a chicken when I was two years old. Maybe it was part of my solution, to forget about him for all the pain that he caused me by dying. Weeks after the confirmation of his death, my older brother and I were still sitting outside our bamboo house, waiting for my father to come home. I made myself believe that at any moment he would come walking down the dirt road, pick me up, hold me in his arms, and make all the pain go away. My father spoiled me. My mother tells me of the time in Thailand when I fell by a pile of rocks and my older sisters tried to help me up and get me back home, but I refused. Each time they carried me home, I would run, crying, back to the same place where I had fallen. I refused to go home until my father came and picked me up. Most fathers would have been furious at their child for such public displays, but my father just smiled as he carried me back home.

My denial still exists. I imagine my father coming back into my life. Maybe he was rescued when they left him there. It's possible. He wasn't dead, and there could be a chance that he was taken to a nearby hospital and his leg was amputated. He tried to look for us and couldn't find us because we had gone to America. He had to get married because he was lonely and thought we had abandoned him. After his papers were completed and approved, he came to America and is still looking for us.

I search the crowds during the Hmong New Year celebrations hoping to find him, but there are very few men in their sixties who have lost a leg or are even crippled. I search the crowds for any man in his sixties who might look like this old wallet picture, but the picture was taken almost twenty-two years ago. My foolish denial reaches its pinnacle when I get suspicious because some old man is nice to my family and resembles the picture of my father. I start wondering about his background and ask many questions, mostly in my head. I probably scare off these men with my curious stares.

In some aspects, I am still the child I was twenty years ago, not wanting to accept my father's death but still hoping. I have found that the more I write about my father, the more questions I have. Many of these questions, I know, can't be answered by anyone but my father. In my writings, I'm piecing together the tangible facts with the imagined facts, hoping to bring my father to life. I know that this exercise is meant to fill a void in my life, and I'm doing it with the certain and familiar things in my life: with words.

Soul Choj Vang ๑

A Tropical Garden in the San Joaquin Valley

In the Fresno backyard
of my subdivision home
enclosed by block and wood
fencing, in the little yardage
of compacted rocky dirt
I co-own with my wife
and the First American Mortgage Co.,
I attempt to recreate
a place that would comfort
the child who continues
to live within me, who
has grown more estranged
and withdrawn with each
new day that I attempt to make
my way into this society.
I try to quiet the child,
to calm his fears with the sounds
that used to lull him to sleep—the whistling
of tropical leaves in the wind.
So I plant bananas, papayas,
lemon grass, elephant grass,
guava, mango, bamboo . . .
They struggle to live
as I scramble to save
and nurture them in this foreign soil,
but the mango died in the summer
heat and the guava died
from the winter freeze.
What remains is a patchy semblance
of the landscape the child was born
into, but it has made him
more than happy to see

some things so comfortingly
familiar, to hear the lullaby
of tropical leaves
played by a worldly wind.
The child is so easy to please,
so innocent, ignoring
the roar of traffic,
of trucks and cars passing at 65 mph,
just over the block fence.

Ꮾ Ꮆ Ꮆ

Chino

In the aisles of men's clothing at Wal-Mart,
I bumped into a little Mexican boy,
maybe four years old. He looked up long at me
in fear, it seemed. Then he put his fingers
on the outside corners of his eyes and pulled
out and up, slanting his eyes.
And he said to me, "Chino! Chino!"
My hand reflexively swung
to wipe out the superior little smile
from the bold brat's face.

But I took hold
of myself. I scrutinized the boy.
His handsome face—a blend
of East and West—was glowing, happy
almost, but the disease had
set in—a meanness already glimmered

in his eyes. My heart ached
for him. I wanted to reach out
and hug him before hate
could eat his soul.
I wanted to say to him: "Yes, little brother, my eyes
are slanted, and rather beautifully, I think.
And yes, I am a Chino, and so are you.
My ancestors came from China,
and so did yours. My many-times-great-grandfather and yours,
they probably played and rode
through the vast steppes together as boys. Maybe
they were even cousins, who cried on each other's shoulders
when yours rode east on the land bridge
and mine was left behind. My little cousin,
who has taught you to hate
a part of yourself so?"

Then his father walked up,
an older version of the boy,
but gnarled like a wind-twisted vine.
He gave me a measuring look,
then a copy of his son's
superior smirk, as if to say:
"I am Spanish: I may look
half Indian, but I'm all
European."

ฅ ฅ ฅ

Letter from the Shore of the Dragon River

1. Letter from the Shore of the Dragon River

So news of you finally reaches me here
on the shore where we used to run and play.
I heard that you had crossed Mekong River
to seek refuge in the land of the Thai.

I heard they put you in a cattle pen
and for a year fed you leftover scraps,
that you lived in little shanties of sticks,
drank water from wells dug next to shitholes.

Now they tell me that you have flown
in a metal eagle into the land of giants.
Are they like in the stories we heard—
do they feed you till you are fat to eat?

Here on the shore of the Dragon River,
nothing has changed, except for your presence.
The river flows calmly in blue summer
and brings raging yellow monsoon currents.

2. In the House of Karst

From my bedroll in this little corner—
my own private space—of the cavern,
I see countless false stars reflect the flame
of my little candle that tries to turn

the gloom of this void into truenight.
I sit here and try to form my thoughts
into a shape, a glowing messenger arrow
that will transcend the vast night sky:

This past season of rain and storms, monsoon
currents turned the Dragon River yellow
and landslides tore the hillsides open
like wounds, our enemies became

our rulers; they overturned heaven
and earth, and drove the survivors
into caverns under the rock mountains we call
the houses of karst. Here in the cool,

vast rooms we share with bats, life is endless
night—the eternal night of the cavern
and the truenights outside that our killers
leave us to roam, and yearn for the day.

3. Sky Soldier on a Mountaintop

From among the broadleaf banana field,
I press the warm metal trigger,
raising death among the enemy camp
just as they sit down to lunch.

When the enemy came to burn us out of the caverns
where we had taken refuge, I came here to join
the Sky Soldiers, hoping their holy rituals
of invincibility would protect me as I learned to kill.

Today, I squeeze off hundreds of rounds
as easily as dropping beads of sweat.
I am a wise old man at fifteen,
knowing that death is nothing.

On the hilltop that is the enemy's
frenzied compound, confusion reigns.
Our bullets hit some, but most
die from their own blind artillery.

The sound of their cries, interrupted
by occasional artillery rounds, is at first chilling,
but the farther we run, the less distinct
they become—they could be mistaken for cries of joy.

It's almost dark now as I sit here
on the top of our mountain and watch
them come to gather their dead
and carry them off like ants trailing back to their hills.

I sit here and watch the Dragon River curve
like a silver ribbon toward you and the setting sun,
smell the sweet odor of burnt flesh,
and wait for the wind to turn.

෧ ෧ ෧

Immunization

We flee through dense bamboo
forests, leaving behind our beds
cluttered with our belongings,
carrying only a bag of rice
and a cook pot tied to a string,
our meager valuables hidden
in a belt of cloth
around our waist. We come
to the river, shed our torn
sandals, and enter the Mekong
with only shreds of our clothing. We float
on inner tubes, trying to cross
to a new land. Our fortunes
suddenly turn worthless
paper, our silver bars
deadly anchor weight.
Finally we come to this
golden land where
father works days and
mother works nights,
while children learn
to live their new life
by watching TV.
How were we to know
that we have come unprepared,
not immunized
against the diseases of this free land—
where sloth, dishonesty,
hatred, and betrayal
are as easy to be infected with,
as deadly
as tropical malaria
was, back home.

Retired

The old Aasics sneaker hangs
awkwardly on the branch,
next to ripe peaches
in the Fresno backyard.
It's a formless clump, almost
unidentifiable. Its once-shiny
purple racing stripes are torn or meshed
into the color of mud.
Looking at it, it's hard
to imagine that the sneaker and its missing mate
once belonged to the Six-Hundred-Mile Club
of the U.S. Seventh Army in Europe.
They trotted those hundreds of miles together,
eating the grainy soil of Germany.
They explored old castles
and stepped on the toes
of centuries-old ghosts.
They walked on the rubble
of the Berlin Wall, feeling
the sharp ruins of an idea still trying
to prick through their soles.
They stepped over the torn
curtain of iron that had turned velvet
and ran a marathon through the old
cobblestone streets of Prague,
where the people had found
renewed vision in the Russian tanks
painted in laughing pink.

They even traveled to Auschwitz, Poland,
where all the participants are gone, but
where one side's power and the other's will
remain—in the piles of clippings
of hair and shoes
refusing to rot.

ဖာ ဖာ ဖာ

The American

In the quiet shades of the evening,
a cool Atlantic wind blows,
bringing a hint of salt,
dispersing the long day of summer heat.
I take a break from the marching
boots in snap-steps, shining
like mirrors flashing, uniforms
spit-shined with colors—gold,
red, white, blue—laid
in a dark field of green, seemingly perfect
rows of white crosses clouding
the rolling hills, decorated
with American flags. I stroll
in the middle of a little Belgian
town that has seen American GIs
come on their yearly pilgrimage
of salute to these holy hills,
where their comrades had fallen
in two world wars.

I, however, out of uniform,
must be something
they don't quite expect
in an American—not Johnson Blonde,
or Varnado Black, or even Chavez Brown.
I can pass for a World War II
Japanese, or I could be
a Chinese who has come
to open a restaurant, or maybe
even a Vietnamese refugee
escaping by boat from his homeland
to seek shelter in France
or here in Belgium.

The old lady, closing the door
to her jewelry
shop, doesn't know
what to make of me. But
she greets me tentatively in English,
and asks where I'm from.

"The U.S.," I answer. She pauses. "Oh!
you must be with the American soldiers."
When I answer, "Yes," she is happy.
"We were at the ceremony today."
She invites me in, to a room
in the back of the shop, hidden,
a secret chamber
for resistance fighters,
spies, and soldiers downed
behind enemy lines.
I am ushered to a hearth
surrounded by three old couples
enjoying their memories,

revived with the flickering fire
and the taste of good coffee.
They greet me with smiles
and invite me to a seat in their circle.

They have an American friend, they tell me,
whom they visit yearly in Pennsylvania.
Their friend had been a pilot,
shot down, wounded, lost and helpless,
until rescued by these people,
who must have been young lovers
then, filled with the juices of fighting
for their lives.

They welcome me, I think,
as a member of the brethren
of their American friend.
I accept their extended grace, their rich coffee,
their fresh cookies, the warmth
of their fire. I don't mind,
when I think of my many American years,
exploring strip malls, supermarkets,
and department stores, without
ever seeing an American hearth
or tasting homemade apple pie.

I tell them my Hmong-American story
of being born on Sky Mountain, fleeing
across the Mekong, living
in the refugee camp, coming to America,
and joining the U.S. Army—
knowing one day
I'll be asked to prove I am
American.

Hawj Xiong ✤

The Last Walk

The last time I talked to him, he was so alive and full of energy. He talked so much, asking me questions, one coming after another as if his natural silence and quietness had disappeared. Although he was only fifty years old, he looked like he was seventy. One could easily notice the wrinkles on his face from a distance. The lines had grown big and deep. He must have gotten them from working in the field back in the old country, I thought to myself.

"You are back," he said to me, as if he did not know that I came home for spring break.

"Yes, Grandfather," I replied. Although he was not my real grandfather, he was an elder in the clan, and I addressed him by that title out of respect.

"How is school?" he asked.

"School is great!" I replied, even though I was failing biology.

"I am glad to hear that you are doing good in school," he said sincerely. He encouraged me to study hard so that someday I would be able to help my family. I was happy that he had come to value education and could see what the future held for me even though it was hard for me to envision it myself.

"Life here is like a prison," he stated, making sure I heard him.

"I know what you mean, Grandfather." I sympathized with him for the struggles he had been through, for I cannot imagine myself in his place.

"It must be hard not speaking English and not knowing how to drive," I said to him. I could do nothing but give him the consolation of my comfort and the warmth of my helpless words.

I know how hard life was for him because I have seen what a usual day entails. Every day starts early. The days are so long and empty, it's hard to envision their end; the days are so boring and lonely, it's impossible to bear the pain. Since the death of his wife a year ago, he has suffered greatly. After her death, it seemed as if the house was transformed by darkness and silence.

He was up by the time the children were ready to go to school. To bear the loneliness and boredom, he turned on the television, switching the channels, trying to make sense of what was happening, only to discover that he had no clue. Feeling out of touch, he turned it off. If he got too bored, he would take a walk to the nearest store, not for the purpose of buying things but for the sake of wasting time. Once in the store, he walked slowly through the aisles, glancing at the colorful ties, sweaters, and shoes on the shelves. "They are beautiful," he said to himself. He wouldn't stop browsing until he bumped into somebody. People apologized by saying, "Excuse me," expecting a reply to come out of his mouth. He remained silent and then walked away as if that person had intentionally insulted him. He did not understand what they were saying.

He noticed other people's physical appearances: height, long noses, the white, black, and blonde hairs of the people around him. He was fascinated by their languages; the sounds of *s, z,* and *r* astounded him. "It would be so nice for one to be able to speak like that," he thought to himself. As the store got more crowded, he realized it was time to go home. Once in the house, he glanced at the big clock hanging on the wall next to two posters from Rainbow Foods. It read 2:00 P.M.

The house was empty and silent, for the children had not returned from school. Bearing the boredom, he would call his few friends on the phone and invite them over to his house, where they played cards and conversed with one another. It seemed as if they were interested only in the past. Sentences and words such as "When I was in Laos . . ." or "In the refugee camps . . ." filled their conversations with memories and tears. They all knew who they were and where they came from; their memories still remained with them and rose in front of them, painfully clear, proving that they had forgotten nothing. When darkness came, his friends left and it was time for him to go to bed.

His nights were filled with nightmares. Sometimes, he screamed in the middle of the night, asking for help. When asked what happened, he replied, "I was in battle." Other times, he dreamed about his daughter who was left behind. In his dreams, he advised her not to come to America because life would be too hard for her. Since arriving in America in 1990, his days have been shattered by loneliness and his nights have been filled with nightmares. He was among thousands who had to escape their country after it had fallen into the hands of the Communists. Like others, for him to start a new life in this country was hard. He became more silent. He did not talk to anybody, not even his own children. Perhaps he was too lonely or maybe he felt that no one understood him.

There was so much pain hidden within him that he decided to take a final walk. One sunny day, about 12:00 noon, while the children were in school, he took the rope that he had been saving for a long time out of the closet and walked to the railroad bridge two blocks away from his house. As he walked toward the bridge, he looked into the distance ahead of him. The road was clear, and it was silent. He was alone. He did not speak or think. He was not worried about the past or the future. The place was peaceful, empty, and silent, and that was all that mattered. He slowly walked toward the bridge, glancing back and forth. When he got to the bridge, he took the rope out of his shirt, carefully tied one end of the rope to the log underneath the bridge, calculating, making sure that his feet would not touch the ground as he let go. Then he made a noose of the other end of the rope and carefully put it around his neck, ensuring that the knot would not loosen as he jumped from the cliff. The final moment came when he took a big breath and let his feet leave the ground. As he struggled for the last breath of air, his body swung back and forth, his face turned blue, and in a matter of seconds he was dead.

Everyone was shocked and frightened when they heard the news. Their faces were darkened with anger and pain. As for me, I did not know what I was supposed to be feeling, and I did not have time to find out. The question was asked—"Why?"—but no one could wait for, much less pursue, an answer. Everyone in the house cried, except me. The worst that could happen had indeed happened, and no one could do anything to stop it. There was no softness anywhere, no bland or soothing element on which to heal myself, to rub the wound.

I wondered if life was much better for him. I wondered if his spirit found its way to the old country so that it could be reincarnated, or if it's still wandering around somewhere in this country because it could not find its way back. Perhaps it has turned into the bad ghost that haunted me at night, turning my peaceful dreams into nightmares. Perhaps the ancestors refused to accept his spirit because they forgot that he was once a good man. They forgot he was a farmer, a husband, a father, a soldier who fought for his country during the Vietnam War.

Moving without tears or speech through a bulge of gray misery, I went out of the house and thought to myself that from now on a new calendar had begun marking time. We will always remember to call his spirit to join us during meager meals. We will always remember to call his spirit to join us during great feasts. The space inside enlarged, and I occupied it fully, tasting the pain, feeling the anger. Too painful. Feeling miserable and at a loss for words, I grabbed my keys and drove to Lake Calhoun, where my mind wandered aimlessly about the clear and gentle surface of the water. I lost the battle to think. The sky cleared and my mind cleared with it.

A folktale told by **Kao Xiong** and translated by **Dia Cha**

The Lovers: A Halloween Tale of Horror

Long ago, a young Hmong man and woman loved each other very much, though they lived in separate villages. Since they were so devoted to one another, the young man made it his custom to visit his girlfriend almost every day. Yet, though they loved each other truly and with all the passion and high hopes of youth, their parents refused to allow them to marry.

One day, the young man set out to work for several days in his family's field, far from the village. He was gone two or three days when, unknown to him, his girlfriend became terribly ill and died.

The young man returned from his chores and mentioned to his parents that he wished to visit his love. The young man's mother and father had no choice but to tell him that while he was gone his girlfriend had been taken by serious illness and, sadly, had already passed away. There would be no more visits to his beloved, they sighed, sharing his sorrow.

Astounded, not wishing to believe his ears, the young man refused to accept what his parents told him.

"No!" he cried. "It's impossible! She was so young. I can't believe it."

Dazed, he ran out of his house and hurried to his girlfriend's village.

Before dark, he came into sight of his young lady's home. It had always been their cherished custom that when he came to call he would pick a banana leaf from one of the many banana trees surrounding the house and blow a musical melody to signal to his love his arrival. This he now did, and his heart swelled with happiness to see that, as always, his girlfriend appeared to him.

Seating herself on the porch outside her house, the girl combed her long, black hair with regular strokes and waited for him, gesturing him to come along.

"It's not yet dark, beloved," he called to her. "And I am very shy. Usually I come after the sun has set, as you know, but today I—"

He stopped, not knowing quite how to broach the subject of the news, happily false, that his parents had mentioned to him.

"Well, beloved," he went on, "today I missed you so much I had to hurry over to see you before the usual time. Now, as we have done so many times before, let's wait until it's dark," he signaled to her, "then I'll come to see you."

With that, the girl waved and returned to the house to wait for him.

When at long last the lengthening shadows of evening had brought on the inky darkness of a jungle-new-moon night, the young lover eagerly entered his girlfriend's house.

As always, she sat by the family's fire pit, but, surprisingly, no fire was burning. The house was dark, and he could make out only the outline of his love where she sat by the cold hearth. Except for the girl, the house was completely deserted.

"Beloved," he called softly in the darkness, "you should start a fire."

"You should do it," she replied. "I am very shy and cannot bring myself to put an end to the darkness that shelters my modesty."

"It is not my home," he answered. "So politeness dictates that I must be more shy than you. It is your house and therefore you should start a fire."

Bowing to his request, the girl set out the kindling in the pit and struck a spark. As the tinder caught flame, she blew on the wood, but the fire refused to start. All remained in blackness.

Still he encouraged her to continue, and she tried once more. This time, as she blew on the flaring tinder, he saw her face briefly. But rather than the familiar features he loved so well, he noted some ineffable alteration in the girl's aspect as the flame flickered and died once more. There was something in her face that was not as it had been, and his heart began to tremble with an uncomfortable suspicion.

Yet again, she struck the spark, and this time the tinder flared up brightly, catching fire. The flames in the pit began to rise, and soon the wood crackled as it burned, shedding light all around. Then, at last, he saw her face fully revealed. It was swollen and pale, while her eyes were black. Casting a quick glance all around the walls, where the fire's flames threw shadows dancing like drunken devils, then back to his beloved, he felt the small hairs on the back of his neck stand up as he saw that the girl was dressed in burial clothes.

Seeing his surprise, she smiled at him to ease his discomfort, but his horror only increased as her dried and deeply cracked lips stretched tight over yellowing teeth. Her garment, the traditional white funeral skirt with long red and green sashes, was dotted all over with blood, and, for the first time, he could detect the smell of decay about her.

Hanging in the middle of the room were two *qeej* and the funeral drum used to communicate with the dead and the spirits, while the rudimentary catafalque, made from bamboo, still hung along the back wall. Indeed, it appeared his beloved had risen from the dead to come and sit with him by the fire pit.

Taking all of this in, the young man shook uncontrollably.

"What's wrong, my beloved?" the young woman asked, her pale, colorless lips split in a ghastly rictus.

"I—I—Beloved," the young man blurted, "where are your parents?"

"Oh, they went to the field," she replied.

In fact, they had run away in the middle of her funeral. Three days after her death, in the middle of the night, her family had been performing funeral rites for her. Her body had begun to decay, yet she opened her eyes wide and sat up, turning her gaze upon them. Then she rose up, and, as they recoiled in horror, she advanced as if to pursue them. With shrieks of absolute terror, they had all run away.

"What's wrong, my beloved," the girl asked again. "Why are you shaking?"

"My—My love," the terrified young farmer stammered, "I—I have to go outside and pee."

"Oh, you can pee in the house," she told him, her black eyes searching his to uncover his intentions. "You don't need to go outside."

"But I'm shy, since we're only boyfriend and girlfriend," he protested. "Please just let me go to pee."

She thought for a moment, seeming somewhat suspicious, but finally said, "Well, if you insist on going outside, then let me tie my sashes around your waist to make sure you don't run away."

To this he agreed, and they stood together. As she tied her sashes to his waist, her hand brushed his wrist, and his knees grew weak to feel her skin, which was as cold as ice.

"Beloved," he called over his shoulder, as he walked out of the house, "when I'm finished, I'll call you and you may pull in the sashes. But please don't pull until I call you. I may not be finished yet."

So saying, he left the house, walked a short distance into the darkness, tied the sashes to a house pole, and ran away as fast as he could.

The spectral girl, meanwhile, continued to wait. But although she waited for a long time, still he did not call her. At last she grew impatient and cried out his name. She cried out his name again and then a third time. There was no answer, and, although she pulled on her sashes, she could not pull them back.

Curious, she went outside to find her sashes tied to a house pole. With a scream that echoed throughout the deserted house and reverberated from the surrounding trees, a scream of anguish, sadness, loneliness, and rage, she leapt into the air.

As she did so, she was suddenly transformed into a ghostly mist that flew through the air in pursuit of her love.

The young man had been moving quickly, however, and he ran to a house in the village of the neighboring Khmu tribe. His face was ashen, he was shaking all over, and he was unable to say a word, merely falling down in the middle of the common-room floor.

The owner of the house, who had been sitting and smoking his pipe, was astonished at this development. However, he realized the poor young man must be in serious difficulty, so he placed a huge wine steamer over him and then waited by the door.

Swift as a bird through the night air, the ghostly woman arrived at the outskirts of this village and changed her form once again, this time to that of a beautiful lady. She traced her beloved's footprints to the house he sought shelter in and soon arrived at the door.

She called out to the owner to appear, and the old man came to the door and smiled.

"Good evening, old man," she said in the lilting tones appropriate to the beautiful form she had assumed. "I seek my boyfriend, who, after a minor disagreement, has run away from me. Have you seen him?"

The old man had seen much life and knew what it was for young lovers to quarrel. For this reason, he almost gave away the hiding place of the young man, in the belief he could help the two patch things up. But something in him hesitated, and instead he replied, "No, young lady. I'm afraid I haven't seen this fellow."

"Old man," she said, "you toy with me. I traced his footsteps to this very house."

The old man was about to speak, tempted yet again to reveal the younger farmer's hiding place in the hope of seeing a happy ending, when the woman continued.

"I warn you, you old fool," she hissed, as anger rose within her and her eyes flashed black, "I will make you pay if you do not tell me the truth."

At this the old man could see there was something not at all right here. He did not mind threats, for he had lived a long life, his children were all grown and married, his wife had died years before, and he was hoping to be reunited with her. Thus he said, "Young lady, we all have footprints hereabouts. It's not only your boyfriend who does. I think you're mistaken and you'd better be off. Good night to you."

Brokenhearted, she turned and left the old man. Arriving at the village outskirts, she changed into a ghost again and was chased into the dark, lonely jungle by the village dogs.

At last the old man removed the wine steamer from over the young man.

"Who was that?" he asked the young farmer.

But the younger man could say nothing, so frightened was he still, and merely shook his head and shrugged.

"Well, then, never mind, young fellow," said the old man. "I've sent her away, and you should be safe now. On your way and home with you."

The young farmer thanked the old man for his protection and left for home and the comfort and security of his family.

Yet the story goes that within a few days he became terribly ill, and soon after that he, too, died. The last words he uttered, before the final breath left his body, were, "Hello, beloved. . . ."

Pa Xiong ೧

broken

I watched her break
for three years I watched her break apart
I watched him hurt her
verbalizing and emotionalizing scars
into her childhood
and her womanhood
I watched her stay day after day
without understanding how much
strength that must have taken
I watched her receive three years of his fists
three years of blue and purple
around her neck
and in her heart
and I watched

when she walked away
with her two-year-old
clutched tightly in her arms
I watched too
and I cried

೧ ೧ ೧

Running Away from Home

i'm homeless
didn't you know?
I never saw my mountains
my jungles, my fields of opium
my home built by my father's two hands

I left before I was even born.

born into a refugee camp
my eyes saw everything
the dirt, the water wells
the women quarreling over who got more rice
little dirty kids trading in bones for candy
my eyes saw
but my mind won't let me remember

Doesn't matter . . . I left that too.

raised in Long Beach
childhood memories of little white kids
calling me names
eating American lunches with ketchup
and Hmong dinners with peppers so hot
I cried every night

But I left that too . . .

"Can't take another earthquake," my mother said.

So we ran away, again.

to Porterville
voted the "All-American Town"
veterans, yellow ribbons, flags everywhere
"Vote for Bush" posters still displayed in some shop windows

But I, I left that too.

the town was too little
I was suffocating
the people too ignorant
it made me hate
the parents too hard
it left me with scars
and the hot summers
well, one hundred and twelve degrees
of heat was killing me
I felt displaced
confined and lost
'cause I knew
I know
i'm homeless . . .

So I left.

I ran
    and I ran
        and I just
            kept running . . .

The Green House

Grandpa died a couple of months ago
and mother is always depressed
so I returned home
to the green house
now almost empty
here I live as I did
a long, long time ago
some days I forget how old I am
some days I don't want to remember
in this green house
I am their quiet
perfect daughter
innocent still, innocent always
I wake up every morning to the crows
of father's roosters
I watch the cows sleep from across the street
all day, all night
and there is no escape
when I am home
I cannot leave this green house
they say the world outside these wooden doors is bad
in this green house
they say I must be Hmong
and I am
without understanding what they mean
they close their eyes when I undress myself
they are deaf when I speak
they clothe me in the old ways that I cannot understand
traditions that have become too heavy

I have worn them on my back for too long
as woman and as child
I know I cannot stay
buried voiceless
I returned home to the green house
only to remind myself why I left in the first place

တ တ တ

Condom Nations

I never understood religion.

I was baptized when I was five, when I didn't even know what
being baptized meant. My family and I became Christians
because the church people wanted to help us. We were refugees,
after all. They even translated sermons into Hmong for us. So
I guess I could say it was a good church. At times it was boring,
though. Oftentimes, I would start talking to the kid next to me
and this Brother would come up behind us and pinch our ears.
He scared all of us kids. Sometimes, the white lady teaching
Sunday school would scare us too. She would tell us that only
144,000 people would go to Heaven and that everyone else,
ever since Adam and Eve, would go to Hell. She said that they
would burn in a river of fire . . . *forever*. That did it to me every
time. I would get sick to my stomach, imagining my body in fire
forever and ever. Sometimes at home, when the stove was hot,
I would touch it really quick just to see how much it would hurt.
And it hurt. I guess Hell would be that feeling, except it would
be all over my body.

Every Sunday, while we folded our hands and closed our
eyes, the evangelist would pray out loud, and I would never

understand what he was trying to say. He kept talking about ghosts with holes and I would just pray that God would help me understand. But I never did. I guess he never heard me, because every Sunday I'd be back in church with my hands folded and my eyes closed, and I'd be confused all over again. So it made me always wonder where he was. After all, he was there to part the Red Sea for Moses; he was there to raise Jesus from the dead; he was there to tell Eve that men shall rule over her. But where was he for me? I prayed every night, with my eyes shut so tight that sometimes they watered and they wouldn't stop. And I would just lie there, waiting for my prayers to be answered. I never asked for much . . . but God, whoever he was, never answered. They told me that he could do anything, but Aaron Williamson in my fifth grade class never liked me, Seree Thao didn't stop kicking me on the school bus, and mommy and daddy never stopped hitting me. And so one night, I just stopped praying. One night, I stopped waiting.

I never understood religion.

Naly Yang ‡

Chapter One

For all the "never afters," reminiscing inspired by growing pains
from 1998 to 2000, one line at a time, in reverse.

In moments of lucidity
Where images merge,
The battle for identity.
Lady—
I have crossed your path
In dreams to idle thoughts
Which charted our journey
Of hands over flesh.
Alas—
What words!
That path not taken
And fools perhaps we be.
I dread the beginnings most
Of passion's language.
I think I skipped chapter one.
And yet,
I miss your lips most of all.

‡ ‡ ‡

In Remembrance

Dedicated to the memory of Bao Lor

The rain was for you
Cleansing a three-year deathwatch—
Two-hour ceremony, abridged.
Bones upon Hmong clothes.
Your blood to span
Across the centuries to come,
Wishing to be remembered
Upon the brush of culture.
One bristle wetted—
How many to make a difference?
Entail a people in flux—
Pictures warped
with the written word.

Life is once, twice, and
yet again.

☩   ☩   ☩

Spirit Trails

My *plig* will always wander,
though many may try to tie it down.
My father, my brother . . .
that is, only until I am wed.
My husband, his family . . .
but what if I do not wed?
No *thaj xwm kab* shall encase my soul.
And should the shaman track and trace,
sounding the spirit gongs to call,
he will not find any spirit trails
although he may walk through spirit doors
and tempt *ntxwg nyoog.*
And if he should try to lay upon my path
a spirit cloth to mark my way
to bring me home,
I will not follow where it leads
for only female spirits linger here.
And the shaman's cloth,
made to bind,
falls not upon my legacy.

Peter Yang *o*

Mother's Day

3 A.M.
a quiet night
the world is sleeping
she is going home
her hands are swollen from chopping celery
her eyes are dry from onion tears
she is tired, but she doesn't complain
the drive home leads straight to her bed
7 A.M.
she wakes to feed her children
dresses them and sends them off to school
then quickly back to bed, for the day is short

12 P.M.
she wakes to have lunch
prepares a meal for the kids, hungry from school
she cleans
3 P.M.
she gathers her things
into the car and off to work
more tiring hours, more swelling and tears
but still no words
she is quiet
she is strong
like the night

o o o

My Dad the Mekong and Me the Mississippi

he fought through a war
helping his clan

I forget the war
not giving a damn

searching the woods
for family that night

searching my mind
for anything right

he crossed the river
nearly drowning for freedom

I've never had
to look for freedom

he crossed a thousand miles
to learn a language he did not know

I crossed no land
yet his language I do not know

remember the past
he says

I can't
I say
I was never meant to be there

join me here
I say

I can't
he says
I was never meant to be here

Kao Yongvang ☙

Is the Beauty Queen a Real Woman?

Editor's Note *In November 1999, Kao participated in the Miss Hmoob 2000 pageant in St. Paul, Minnesota. Out of the twelve contestants, she was contestant number four. This piece is arranged in the order in which the contestants showcased their "gigs" during the talent show portion of the pageant.*

You stare at me
Wondering if I'll be the next queen as I wonder if you'll think
I'm a real woman.

> Snapshot 1
> I come out wearing my father's uniform,
> Shouting for you to remember the fallen ones,
>   the lost ones
> In a war that I cannot comprehend and perhaps
> Don't remember either.

> Snapshot 2
> My hip movements sway with the twist of my wrists
> As I display for you
> How a Hmong woman should really
> Dance.

> Snapshot 3
> Or perhaps, my womanhood is best shown
> By my gentle and sub-miss-ive manners, which are much
> Stronger
> Than you could ever imagine. It's all about balance.

Snapshot 5
Maybe you'll find me exotic
With my hair up in a bun,
My fingers with nine-inch-long nails,
As I dance for you
Barefoot
To the drums of a foreign country.

Snapshot 6
You'd probably think of me as a woman
If I had a pretty face and sang *kwv txhiaj*
With lyrics that you'd find amusing because my soft
    voice sounds so
Cute.

Snapshot 7
But I think that you'd appreciate a woman with culture,
So let me sing you a song in Chinese, in words that you
    cannot understand.
But that doesn't matter because my body-molding dress
Looks good enough.

Snapshot 8
Or should I be more cultivated and perform for you
A dance of incense and wild flowers.
It's a step closer to Kama Sutra, so maybe you'll discover
The real woman
In me.

Snapshot 9

No, let's go back to our origins and dance with
    an umbrella
As we did in the high mountains of China.
If it is the true source of our culture, then
It is the true source of my womanhood.

Snapshot 10

Or being a woman is when I seduce you,
Wearing a slick black dress and tall high heels,
A flower tucked in my hair,
And spreading fans in my hands,
Moving my body to the music of a Latin man.

Snapshot 11

But I come to my senses and show you my true heart:
I'm an Oriental angel
With butterfly wings and rose petals to spread
Good fortune.

Snapshot 12

No, I lied again.
You'll find the woman in me in the song that I sing
In a language that you know and understand.
But I know that even though you're hearing it,
    you're not listening to me.
You're too preoccupied by my tall and lean body,
And your eyes are hypnotized by my moving lips.

Snapshot 4
So, I wonder if you'll see beauty
In the woman sitting on the toilet,
Crying about rape
Because she reminds you of the
Ugliness
Of your sexual fantasies.

Beauty is a woman's attribute, as the winner might tell you.
Let her sing you her tales and charm you with her dances;
Maybe you'll find her imperfect nose and unshapely body
More bearable to look at because they'd spare you
your own query about being a man.

Contributors

BC is the pseudonym of a writer and visual artist who lives in St. Paul, Minnesota. He recieved his B.F.A. from a state university in Kansas, and he describes his writing as simple yet confusing.

Bee Cha attended St. Olaf College in Northfield, Minnesota, and earned his master of architecture degree from Washington University in St. Louis, Missouri. He lives in Madison, Wisconsin, where he works for Flad & Associates as an architectural designer. He has been involved with Hmong Artist Trek, a group that encourages Hmong artists to utilize their skills by participating in community projects. He also volunteered to expose youths living in public housing to the fundamental workings of architecture, assisted in planning for the addition to the St. Paul Hmong Alliance Church, and designed artworks for Hmong American Partnership. In his leisure time, Bee listens to Green Day, watches NBA games, plays chess, and enjoys finger-picking his guitar.

Dia Cha is a professor of anthropology and ethnic studies at St. Cloud State University. She holds a B.A. in anthropology from Metropolitan State College of Denver, an M.A. in applied anthropology from Northern Arizona University, and a Ph.D. from the University of Colorado–Boulder. In addition to scholarly articles and reports, Dia has written *Dia's Story Cloth*, and she is a coauthor, with Dr. Norma Livo, of *Folk Stories of the Hmong* and *Teaching with Folk Stories of the Hmong: An Activity Book*.

True Hang is the pseudonym of a single Hmong woman writer who lives in St. Paul, Minnesota. She graduated from a private four-year college and currently works for a nonprofit organization. Her writings have been published in various local venues. She frequents used bookstores and enjoys sitting in cafés reading and writing for hours on Sundays. If you see her, please don't interrupt her work.

Sharon Her is a writer and consultant. Her awards include participation in the 2000 Loft Asian American Inroads Program, an Asian American Renaissance Emerging Artist Regrant, and a Jerome Travel and Study Grant. Current projects include co-authoring a children's book with David Haynes and developing a Hmong student-needs video with Minnesota Public Schools. In the summer of 2002 she taught youth fiction classes for both SASE: The Write Place! and the Loft. She lives in Minneapolis.

May Lee studies English at the University of Minnesota–Twin Cities and does not intend to become a teacher at any point in her life. She is a playwright, novelist, and short-story writer who aspires to get paid for her work. Her genres of interest include memoir, fiction, romance, and mystery thrillers, as well as explorations of slices of Hmong life. If she could meet one author, it would be Dean Koontz because he actually wrote back to her, in longhand.

Kou Lor lives and works in Fond du Lac, Wisconsin. He has a B.A. in psychology and a B.S. in computer science, both from the University of Wisconsin–Oshkosh. He started writing at the age of fourteen and, while he has been improving his skills since those first days of "Roses are red," he is still searching for his voice as a poet and a Hmong American.

Pacyinz Lyfoung is a community activist and women's issues advocate who hopes to use the power of words to effect social change, to remember what came before us, and to shape what will come after us. Her work has been published in *Paj Ntaub Voice* and the *Asian American Journal,* and she is currently a volunteer coordinator on the River Dragon Tales project, a collection of life experiences and collective wisdom from Asian Pacific Islander women and girls living in Minnesota.

Mai Neng Moua is founder and current editor of *Paj Ntaub Voice.* A poet and creative nonfiction writer, she has been published in *Healing by Heart, Rehabilitation Counseling Bulletin,* the Minneapolis *Star Tribune,* and *We Are the Freedom People.* Mai Neng has a B.A. from St. Olaf College in Northfield, Minnesota, and is completing her M.A. at the Hubert H. Humphrey Institute of Public Affairs at the University of Minnesota. She is the public policy coordinator for the nonprofit organization Institute for New Americans, located in Minneapolis. She loves traveling, international films, and lakes, oceans, and mountains, and she enjoys teaching creative writing to Hmong youth at the Jane Addams School for Democracy. She lives with her mother and two brothers in St. Paul.

Vayong Moua grew up in Eau Claire, Wisconsin, and earned a B.A. in philosophy, sociology/anthropology, and Asian studies from St. Olaf College in Northfield, Minnesota, and an M.P.A. in public policy from the University of Wisconsin–Madison. He has studied abroad in Asia, taught English in Japan, and wandered in Alaska. He currently works as a program manager at Achieve!Minneapolis, an intermediary organization that creates business and community partnerships with Minneapolis public schools. He passionately enjoys disc golf, volleyball, microbreweries, sticky rice, Coldplay, Princess Mononoke, and traveling.

Noukou Thao spent her childhood running around barefoot with her cousins, playing war games, and exploring the bambooed back yards and rivers of Selma, Alabama. After studying film and literature at the University of Wisconsin–Milwaukee, she was drawn to the fast-growing Hmong community in St. Paul–Minneapolis, where for five years she held various grant-writing jobs in the nonprofit sector. She is one of the cofounders of the Center for Hmong Arts & Talent (CHAT). She currently resides in Star Prairie, Wisconsin (population 574), and is applying to various graduate programs in creative writing and folklore. She is working on two novels, *New Mexico Odyssey* and *A Tale of the Mermaid's*.

Bryan Thao Worra is a first-generation Lao-Hmong adoptee. He attended Otterbein College in Ohio to study multicultural communications. He has worked with Asian communities across the United States for a variety of agencies, including Hmong National Development, *Hmong Tribune*, Asian Media Access, and the Hmong Nationality Archives. He is a 2002 artist-in-residence for the Many Voices Program of the Minnesota Playwrights' Center and a strong advocate for the support of community media that meet the community's needs.

Va-Megn Thoj is a community activist and filmmaker. He resides in St. Paul, Minnesota.

Ka Vang was born on Long Cheng, a CIA military base in Laos, just days before the country's fall to communism in 1975. Her family came to the United States five years later. She attended the University of Minnesota and was a reporter for the *St. Paul Pioneer Press* and the *Chicago Tribune*. She was named the 2001 and 2002 recipient of the Many Voices Playwright Fellowship from the Playwrights' Center in Minneapolis. She is also the recipient of the Asian American Renaissance / Jerome Foundation

Artist's Career Development Grant, as well as a Jerome Foundation Study and Travel Grant and a Minnesota State Arts Board Artist Fellowship.

M. S. Vang lives in St. Paul, Minnesota. She studied English and theatre in London and holds a B.A. in English from the University of Minnesota–Twin Cities. She would like to acknowledge Ms. Marty Niemela as the epitome of a high school English teacher.

Mayli Vang is a graduate of the College of St. Catherine in St. Paul, Minnesota. In addition to *Paj Ntaub Voice,* her writings have appeared in *Tilting the Continent: Southeast Asian Writing.*

Soul Choj Vang was born in Laos and came to the United States as a teenager. He spent two years at California State University–Fullerton and then dropped out of college to search for his soul. He served with the U.S. Army in Germany and Texas, after which he returned to California to rejoin Hmong society and continue his education. He recently earned an M.F.A. in creative writing and a secondary teaching credential from California State University–Fresno. He lives with his wife and two daughters in Fresno.

Hawj Xiong is a graduate of Carleton College in Northfield, Minnesota. He is currently working toward an M.B.A. at the University of St. Thomas in St. Paul. He lives with his wife, child, and parents in Brooklyn Park.

Kao Xiong was recruited to become a soldier in 1963 at the age of thirteen by the American CIA in Laos. He served his country and protected his people until 1974 when Laos became a communist regime. He lived in a refugee camp in Thailand for almost three years and then came to the United States in 1978. He has worked as a machine operator and apartment manager. He is recently retired.

Pa Xiong is a graduate of the University of California–Los Angeles. She lives in Diamond Bar, California, and works as an English teacher at a local middle school. She once sold overpriced furniture to the rich and famous in Beverly Hills, and she hopes one day to become a hairstylist.

Naly Yang is the executive director of the Women's Association of Hmong and Lao (WAHL) and a graduate of Carleton College in Northfield, Minnesota. Her work has been published in the anthology *Famous Poets of the Twentieth Century* as well as in local publications. She has taught creative writing to Asian American high school students through the Asian American Renaissance program and also dabbles in nontraditional art forms such as karate and swordsmanship. In her free time, Naly enjoys spending time with family and friends, gardening, and traveling to far-off places in search of inspiration.

Peter Yang does not consider himself to be a "traditional" writer. He often foregoes conventional structures and methods in favor of "feel." He believes the appeal of literary work is not in its scholarly worth but in its value to everyday personal health and growth. A smile, a twinge of pain, an emotion from a reader is the goal and the reward. Presently, he is continuing his work in literature while applying this belief in other fields such as media arts and public speaking. Someday he hopes to become an accomplished writer, filmmaker, and speaker, all the while brandishing a smile. Peter resides in St. Paul, Minnesota.

Kao Yongvang trekked to Minnesota in her quest to understand the diversity of Hmong American identity. After three years in St. Paul, she moved back to California; she now lives in San Francisco. Kao is currently working on a new writing project titled *Reputation,* a compilation of various stories about Hmong women and their reputations within the community. She aspires to become an urban planner for a midsize city and hopes to one day learn how to ride a bicycle.

Notes

Introduction

Text

BC

True Hang

36 **tu siab** A complex Hmong word that means a deep sadness or woundedness in the heart or soul; a deep loneliness, emptiness, or longing. *Tu siab* does not have the negative connotations of depression, however.

38 **cousin-grandmother** a title of respect given to an older member of one's clan

38 **paj ntaub** needlework

39 **They would lose money** refers to the cultural practice of paying compensation to right a wrong

40 **his money to spend** income from being a soldier in the CIA's "Secret War"

41 **ua neeb kho** ceremony performed by a shaman to heal the sick

Mai Neng Moua

57 **Mekong** river separating Laos from Thailand

57 **zaub ntsuab** green vegetable

57 **zaub paj** flower vegetable

63 **Mekas** white Americans

74 **EPO** (erythropoietin) a glycoprotein hormone produced by the kidney that is responsible for the regulation of red blood cell production

Noukou Thao

85 **White Hmong . . . Green dialect** "White" and "Green" refer to the language spoken by different groups and are also linked to visual identity based on women's dress ("White" being white and "Green" being brilliantly colored).

Bryan Thao Worra

97 **Dahmer, Gacy, Speck, Charles Francis Ng** Jeffrey Dahmer, John Wayne Gacy, Richard Speck, and Charles Francis Ng: twentieth-century North American serial killers

99 **Valhalla** Viking paradise for warriors killed in battle

99 **Elysium** Greek paradise

99 **PDJ** French: *Plaines des Jarres:* the principal battlefield during the war in northern Laos

101 **Sun Tzu** the general who wrote *The Art of War,* a classic Chinese text that continues to be used for military and business applications around the world

Bamboo Among the Oaks was designed and set in type by Cathy Spengler, Minneapolis. The typeface is Figural, designed by Oldrich Menhart in 1940. This book was printed by Maple Press, York, Pennsylvania.